Surya Puran: The Radiance of Dharma

(English Edition)

Featuring Original Hindi Verses with English Transliteration and Translation

UNMESHA JENA

Title: Surya Puran- The Radiance of Dharma (English Edition)

Author: Unmesha Jena

ISBN: 978-93-343-5410-2

First Edition: 2025

Printed in India

Preface

The Surya Puran stands as a luminous testament to the timeless reverence humanity has held for the Sun—the giver of life, light, energy, and divine wisdom. Rooted in the rich spiritual traditions of India, this text not only celebrates Surya Dev as a celestial body but as a conscious divine force, guiding humanity toward truth, health, discipline, and liberation.

With deep respect and devotion, I have undertaken the task of translating this sacred text into English, hoping to make its wisdom accessible to a global audience. This translation is not merely linguistic—it is an effort to preserve and convey the spiritual essence, cultural beauty, and devotional rhythm of the original verses.

The Surya Puran, particularly in the version I have translated, unfolds through conversations between Lord Shiva and Goddess Parvati, revealing the profound effects of Surya worship, the power of Sunday fasts, the twelve manifestations of the Sun, and the blessings that flow from faith, devotion, and righteous living. Stories of transformation—from barren women gaining virtuous sons to sinners finding salvation—are not just allegories but living reminders of the divine grace that Surya Dev bestows.

May this humble work serve as a bridge between ancient Vedic devotion and the contemporary seeker's quest for light, wisdom, and inner peace.

With gratitude to the divine light within and around us,
Unmesha Jena
Translator
Surya Puran – English Edition

The Author

The author is an experienced IT Project Manager with a deep-rooted spiritual inclination. Driven by personal devotion to Lord Surya and inspired by His generous heart, she has undertaken the task of translating the *Surya Puran* into English to make its timeless teachings more reachable to today's readers.

She graduated with a Bachelor of Technology degree in 2015, securing the top rank in the Computer Science department. Alongside her professional and academic pursuits, she had been a Classical Odissi dancer for more than 12 years—an experience that reflects her long-standing appreciation for Indian culture, art, and literature.

The purpose behind this translation is to bring forth the *Surya Puran*'s core messages of righteousness, discipline, and spiritual living to a wider audience, transcending linguistic boundaries. The author believes that sharing this wisdom can contribute meaningfully to individual growth and collective well-being by awakening people to the deeper values and true purpose of life.

Acknowledgement

With profound humility and indebtedness, I acknowledge the divine guidance of Lord Surya, whose eternal light has been the inspiration behind this work. It is His grace that illuminated my path and gave me the strength to undertake this sacred translation.

I am deeply thankful to my family, for their unwavering support, patience, and encouragement throughout this journey. Their belief in the spiritual value of this work has been a constant source of motivation.

To the countless sages and scholars who have preserved the Surya Puran across generations, I offer my deepest respect. Their wisdom laid the foundation upon which this translation stands.

To every reader and devotee who turns these pages with reverence, I extend my heartfelt thanks. May His light fill your lives with knowledge and healing.

Last but not the least, to the Divine Couple, without whose sacred dialogue this Puran would not have come into existence — to the Creator, the Nurturer, the Destroyer; to the inseparable Duo, the embodiment of energy and power that governs this universe; the One who is reason enough to pen down this book — Lord Shiva and Maa Parvati.

Table of Contents

CHAPTER 1
THE POWER OF FAITH AND DEVOTION

(Mahābandhyāstrī Varṇana Nāma Prathamo'dhyāyaḥ)
– The miraculous result of Surya worship for barren women

This chapter opens the sacred *Surya Puran* with invocations to Lord Ganesha, Lord Vishnu, Goddess Gauri, and Lord Surya, establishing a tone of deep devotion and reverence. The narrative emphasizes the immense power, radiance, and benevolence of Surya Dev—the Sun God—who is portrayed as the eternal source of light, wisdom, and spiritual strength.

The core message of this chapter centers on the miraculous grace of Surya in blessing a barren woman with five virtuous, powerful sons through sincere devotion. It describes the specific observances she follows: fasting on Sundays, listening to the *Surya Puran*, feeding Brahmins, chanting Surya's name, and maintaining a lifestyle of dharma and discipline. The chapter assures that such unwavering devotion to Surya removes obstacles like infertility and leads to both material and spiritual rewards.

Through poetic verses and divine dialogue, this chapter illustrates Surya's role as a healer, guide, and bestower of boons—highlighting the power of faith, ritual purity, and regular worship. It sets the foundation for the Purana's deeper teachings, inviting the reader into a path of devotion and divine connection.

The Blessing for a Barren Woman

卐 श्रीगणेशाय नमः 卐

卐 Shri Ganeshaya Namah 卐

I bow to Shri Ganesha, the remover of obstacles.

दो०- बंदि कंजपद जोरि कर, श्रीपति गौरि गणेश।
तुलसिदास कहते सुजश, वरणौं कथा दिनेश ।।
Doha (Couplet):
Bandi kanjapad jori kar, Shripati Gauri Ganesh,
Tulsidas kahate sujash, varanauṁ kathā Dinesh.

I bow with folded hands to the lotus feet of Vishnu (Shripati), Gauri (Parvati), and Ganesh,
Tulsidas now speaks the divine glories—he begins the tale of Dinesh (the Sun God).

बन्दौं चरण हृदय धरि, प्रेम भक्ति मन लाय।
महिमा अगम अपार है, साहब ज्ञान सहाय ॥
Bandauṁ charan hṛiday dhari, prem bhakti man lāy,
Mahimā agam apār hai, sāhab jñān sahāy.

I bow at His feet, placing them in my heart, with love and devotion in mind,
His greatness is immeasurable and boundless—He is the Lord who grants wisdom and guidance.

सूर्य देवता सुमिरौं तोही ।
सुमिरत ज्ञान बुद्धि देहु मोही ।
Invocation to Surya:
Sūrya Devatā sumiraum̐ tohi,
Sumirat jñān buddhi dehu mohi.

O Surya Deva, I remember and meditate upon You—
By remembering You, bless me with knowledge and wisdom.

ज्योति स्वरूप भानु बलवाना ।
तेज प्रताप है अग्नि समाना ॥
Jyoti svarūp Bhānu balavānā,
Tej pratāp hai agni samānā.

You are the radiant form, O mighty Bhanu (Sun),
Your brilliance and power are like blazing fire.

तुम आदित्य परमेश्वर स्वामी ।
अलख निरंजन अन्तर्यामी ॥
Tum Āditya Parameshwar Swāmī,
Alakh Niranjan antar-yāmī.

You are Aditya, the Supreme Lord and Master,
Invisible, pure, and the knower of all hearts.

बरनि न जाइ ज्योति कर लीला ।
धर्म धुरन्धर परम सुशीला ॥
Barani na jāi jyoti kar līlā,
Dharm dhurandhar param suśīlā.

Your radiant play (leela) cannot be fully described in words,
You are the upholder of dharma and embodiment of supreme virtue.

ज्योति कला चहुँ ओर बिराजै ।
जगमग कानन कुंडल साजै ॥
Jyoti kalā chahum̐ or birājai,
Jagmag kānan kuṇḍal sājai.

Your divine light spreads in all directions,
Adorning the universe like glittering earrings in a luminous forest.

नील बरन वर है असवारी ।
ज्ञान विधान धर्म व्रतधारी ॥
Nīl baran var hai asvārī,
Jñān vidhān dharm vratadhārī.

He is blue-hued and rides a noble chariot,
The embodiment of knowledge, order, dharma, and observance of vows.

तासु कथा मैं कहौं बखानी ।
पुरुषोत्तम आनन्दघन ज्ञानी ॥
Tāsu kathā main kahauṁ bakhānī,
Puruṣottam ānandghan jñānī.

I shall now describe His divine story—
He is Purushottam, the supreme being, full of bliss and wisdom.

आदित महिमा अगम अपारा ।
तीन भुवन जेहि रवि उजियारा ॥
Ādit mahimā agam apārā,
Tīn bhuvan jehi Ravi ujiyārā.

The glory of Aditya (the Sun) is unfathomable and limitless,
He illuminates all three worlds with His radiant light.

दो०- आदित कथा पुनीत अति, गावहिं शंभु सुजान ।
तीन लोक छवि ज्योतिमय, करौं प्रताप बखान ॥
Doha (Couplet):
Ādit kathā puneet ati, gāvahiṁ Śambhu sujān,
Tīn lok chhavi jyotimay, karoṁ pratāp bakhān.

The sacred story of Aditya is sung by wise ones like Lord Shiva,
His brilliance lights the three worlds—I now recount His divine power.

सुनहु उमा आदित परतापा ।
बरनौं बिमल सूर्य कर जापा ॥
Sunahu Umā Ādit pratāpā,
Barnaūṁ bimal Sūrya kar jāpā.

Listen, Uma, to the mighty power of Aditya,
I shall now describe the pure chanting and praise of Surya.

नाथ महातम सुनहु भवानी ॥
कहौं पुनीत कथा शुभ बानी ॥
Nāth mahātam sunahu Bhavānī,
Kahauṁ puneet kathā śubh bānī.

O Bhavani, hear this divine greatness of the Lord,
I speak to you this sacred tale in auspicious words.

बाँझ सुने एक मास पुराना ।
मन क्रम बचन धरे व्रत ध्याना ॥
Bāṁjh sune ek mās Purānā,
Man, karam, vachan dhare vrat dhyānā.

If a childless woman listens to this Purana for one month,
With pure thoughts, actions, words, and firm devotion to the vow—

द्वादश मास करे इतवारा ।
नेम धर्म एक मधुर अहारा ॥
Dvādaś mās kare itavārā,
Nema dharm ek madhur ahārā.

And observes Sunday fasts for twelve months,
Eating only a simple and sweet meal, and following dharma sincerely.

कुश बिछाय करे विश्रामा ।
हर्षित जपे सूर्य कर नामा ॥
Kush bichhāy kare viśrāmā,
Harṣit jape Sūrya kar nāmā.

Spreading Kusha grass, she sits and rests peacefully,
Joyfully chanting the names of Lord Surya.

आदित वासर जबहीं आवै ।
सुनै पुरान अरु विप्र जिमावै ॥
Ādit vāsar jabahīṁ āvai,
Sunai Purān aru vipra jimāvai.

On every Sunday (Ādityvār),
She listens to the Surya Purana
and feeds the Brahmins.

इतनी टेक धरे तिय जबहीं ।
होहिं दयालु दयानिधि तबहीं ॥
Itnī ṭek dhare tiya jabahīṁ,
Hohiṁ dayālu Dayānidhi tabahīṁ.

When a woman holds such
steadfast devotion,
The compassionate Lord Surya,
the ocean of mercy, blesses
her.

होहि पाँच सुत अग्नि समाना ।
धर्म धुरन्धर ज्ञान निधाना ॥
Hohiṁ pāñc sut agni samānā,
Dharma dhurandhar jñān nidhānā.

She will bear five sons, radiant
like fire,
Strong in dharma and rich in
divine knowledge.

तिनसों जीत सके नहिं कोई।
विद्यावान सुलक्षण होई ॥
Tinasoṁ jīt sake nahiṁ koī,
Vidyavān sulakṣaṇ hoī.

No one will be able to defeat
them,
They will be learned, virtuous,
and full of auspicious qualities.

दो०- बाँझ कथा मनलाय के, टेक धरै व्रत ध्यान ।
निश्चय उपजे पाँच सुत, योद्धा अग्नि समान ॥
Doha (Couplet):
Bāṁjh kathā manlāy ke, ṭek dharai vrat dhyān,
Niśchay upaje pāñc sut, yoddhā agni samān.

If a barren woman listens with devotion, holds firm to fasting and meditation,
She will surely bear five sons, all of them warriors like fire.

इति श्री सूर्यमहाबंध्यास्त्रीवर्णनोनाम प्रथमोऽध्यायः ॥
Iti Shri Sūrya Mahābandhyāstrī Varṇanonāma Prathamo'dhyāyaḥ.

Thus ends the first chapter of the Surya Mahapurana,
Titled *"The Description of the Great Blessing for a Barren Woman."*

CHAPTER 2
THE RADIANCE THAT HEALS

(Mahākuṣṭha Varṇana Nāma Dvitīyo'dhyāyaḥ)

– How devotion to Surya cures incurable diseases.

This chapter highlights the healing power of Lord Surya, particularly His divine ability to cure severe diseases like leprosy (*kuṣṭha*). It begins with a continuation of the reverent dialogue, emphasizing how simply listening to the glories of Surya with faith can initiate a process of physical and spiritual purification.

The chapter prescribes a set of devotional practices for those afflicted with chronic or incurable ailments—especially leprosy. These include fasting on Sundays (Ravi-var), consuming food without salt, offering fragrant flowers in leaf bowls, performing sacred fire rituals (*homa*) in the name of Surya, and applying the resultant holy ash on the body. Through these actions, the devotee aligns body, mind, and soul in sacred discipline.

The text assures that by following this path of devotion with sincerity, one will not only be rid of disease but will also receive the gift of health, vitality, and divine protection. The chapter reaffirms Surya as a compassionate and omniscient deity whose blessings can transform suffering into strength.

Ultimately, Chapter 2 teaches that unwavering faith in Surya, combined with disciplined practice, can restore wholeness and well-being even in the face of grave afflictions.

The Removal of Leprosy by Surya's Grace

कथा कहौं रवि अमृत बानी ।
मन स्थिर करि सुनहु भवानी ॥
Kathā kahaun ravi amrit bānī I
Man sthir kari sunahu Bhavānī II.

Now I shall tell you the nectar-like tale of Lord Surya,
O Bhavani, listen with a steady and focused mind.

कुष्ठ बरन हो जाके अंगा ।
सुनै मनुज सो भानु प्रसंगा ॥
रवि दिन भोजन करै अलोना ।
पुष्प सुवास चढ़ावै दोना ॥
विप्र बोलाइ रवि होम करावै ।
सोइ भस्म लै अंग लगावै ॥
निश्चय कुष्ठ बरन छय जाई ।
धनि महिमा है सूर्य गोसाँई ॥
Kuṣṭha baran ho jāke angā,
Sunai manuj so Bhānu prasangā.
Ravi din bhojan karai alonā,
Puṣpa suvās chaṛhāvai donā.
Vipra bolāi Ravi hom karāvai,
Soi bhasma lai ang lagāvai.
Niśchay kuṣṭha baran chhaya jāī,
Dhani mahimā hai Sūrya Gosāī.

Whose body is afflicted by leprosy or skin disease,
That person should listen to the glories of the Sun (Bhanu).
On Sundays, eat food without salt,
And offer fragrant flowers in leaf bowls.
Call a Brahmin and perform a fire ritual (homa) for the Sun,
And apply the sacred ash from it on the body.
Surely, the affliction of leprosy will be removed—
Such is the glorious power of Lord Surya!

दो०- जाके कुष्ठ शरीर में, सो नित सुनै पुरान ।
निश्चयं सूर्य प्रताप से, पावै काया दान ॥
Doha (Couplet):
Jāke kuṣṭha śarīr mein, so nit sunai purān,
Niśchayaṁ Sūrya pratāp se, pāvai kāyā dān.

One whose body suffers from leprosy should daily listen to this Purana.
Surely, by the grace of Surya, they will be gifted a healthy body.

इतिश्री सूर्यमहाकुष्ठवर्णनोनाम द्वितीयोऽध्यायः ॥
Iti śrī Sūrya-Mahākuṣṭha-Varṇano Nāma Dvitīyo'dhyāyaḥ.

Thus ends the second chapter titled "*The Description of Major Leprosy by the Sun God*".

CHAPTER 3
THE LIGHT FOR THE BLIND

(Andhalochanaprāpti Nāma Tṛtīyo'dhyāyaḥ)
– Surya's power to restore vision and remove darkness.

This chapter of the *Surya Puran* unveils the miraculous healing powers of Lord Surya, especially in curing ailments of the body and mind. Narrated by Lord Shiva to Goddess Parvati (Bhavani), the tale begins with a call to attentively listen to the glories of Surya. It is said that those suffering from skin discoloration, leprosy, or even congenital blindness can be healed through steadfast devotion to the Sun God.

The chapter prescribes spiritual discipline, such as fasting on five consecutive Sundays, consuming only sweet and simple food, applying sandalwood and agar paste to the body, and meditating upon Surya with sincerity. Those who listen or recite this sacred tale with a pure heart—especially under a Peepal tree—are assured of recovery, even from incurable diseases.

It emphasizes that even a person blind from birth can gain eyesight and relief from sorrow through devotion, faith, and spiritual practice. This narrative highlights the compassionate grace of Surya, whose divine energy uplifts the suffering and restores wholeness through sacred discipline and unwavering faith.

Restoring Sight and Health through Devotion

सूर्य कथा मैं कहौं बखानी ।
मन स्वतन्त्र करि सुनहु भवानी ॥
जाके बरन अंग मह होई ।
सूर्य-कथा पाठ कर सोई ॥

Sūrya kathā maiṁ kahauṁ bakhānī,
Man svatantra kari sunahu Bhavānī.
Jāke baran aṅg maha hoī,
Sūrya-kathā pāṭh kara soī.

Now I narrate the detailed tale of Surya,
Listen freely and attentively, O Bhavani.
Whoever has discoloration on their limbs,
Should recite or listen to the tale of Surya.

करे पाँच व्रत नर इतवारा ।
नेम धर्म इक मधुर अहारा ॥
चन्दन अगर लेप तन करई ।
निशि दिन ध्यान सूर्य पर धरई ॥
निश्चय अंग बरन मिट जाई ।
धनि महिमा है सूर्य गोसाँई ॥
भानु चरित्र सुनै मन लाई ।
निश्चय कुष्ठ बरन छय जाई ॥

Kare pāñc vrat nar itavārā,
Nema dharma ik madhur ahārā.
Chandan agar lep tan karaī,
Nishi din dhyān Sūrya par dharaī.
Niśchay aṅg baran miṭ jāī,
Dhani mahimā hai Sūrya Gosāī.
Bhānu charitra sunai man lāī,
Niśchay kuṣṭh baran chhaya jāī.

If a person observes five fasts on Sundays,
With discipline and devotion, and takes simple, sweet food,
Applies sandalwood and agar paste on the body,
And meditates daily on Lord Surya—
Surely, skin ailments and discoloration will vanish.
Such is the divine glory of Lord Surya!
He who listens with full devotion to the tales of Bhanu (Surya),
Will certainly be freed from leprosy and all skin diseases.

दो०- जाके उपजै कुष्ठ तन, सो नित सुनै पुरान ।
धन महिमा आदित्य की, करौं प्रताप बखान ॥
Doha (Couplet):
Jāke upjai kuṣṭh tan, so nit sunai purān,
Dhan mahimā Āditya kī, karauṁ pratāp bakhān.

He whose body suffers from leprosy should listen daily to this Purana.
Glory be to Aditya (Surya); now I shall narrate His divine power.

सूर्य-कथा मैं कहौं बुझाई ।
मन क्रम बचन सुनिय चितलाई ॥
जो नर होइ अन्धयुग लोचन ।
सो यह कथा सुनै दुखमोचन ॥
करै लोन बिन एक अहारा ।
विविध भाँति कर नेम अचारा ॥
Sūrya-kathā maiṁ kahauṁ bujhāī,
Man kram vacan suniya citlāī.
Jo nar hoi andhayug locan,
So yah kathā sunai duḥkamocan.
Karai lon bin ek ahārā,
Vividh bhānti kar nem achārā.

I now explain the tale of Surya with clarity—
Listen to it with focused heart, actions, and words.
Even one who has been blind since birth,
If he listens to this tale, his sorrows will be removed.
He should eat a single meal without salt,
And follow various forms of discipline and ritual practice.

पीपर तरु तर सुनै पुराना ।
पावै लोचन अन्ध सुजाना ॥
अन्धा लोचन निश्चय पावै ।
जो यह कथा सुचित मन गावै ॥
Pīpar taru tar sunai purānā,
Pāvai locan andh sujānā.
Andhā locan niścay pāvai,
Jo yah kathā sucit man gāvai.

If one listens to this Purana while sitting under a Peepal tree (sacred fig tree),
Even a wise person born blind shall receive eyesight.
Surely, a blind person will gain vision,
If he sings or recites this tale with a pure and devoted heart.

दो०- अन्ध लहै निश्चय नयन, जो जाने प्रभु एकं ।
पुलकित परम पुनीत यह, धरे कथा पर टेक ॥
Doha (Couplet):
Andh lahai niśchay nayan, jo jāne prabhu ekaṁ,
Pulakit param punīt yah, dhare kathā par ṭek.

Certainly, the blind shall gain eyes if they realize the One Supreme Lord.
This sacred tale brings divine joy to those who place their full faith in it.

इतिश्री महासूर्य अन्धलीचनप्राप्तोनाम तृतीयोऽध्यायः ॥
Iti śrī Mahāsūrya Andhalocanaprāptonāma Tṛtīyo'dhyāyaḥ.

Thus ends the third chapter titled *"The Granting of Eyesight by the Great Surya."*

Chapter 4
Fulfilment of all Desires

(Manovāñchita Dātā Nāma Chaturtho'dhyāyaḥ)
– How Surya fulfills devotees' heartfelt wishes.

This chapter from the *Surya Puran* beautifully illustrates the compassionate nature of Lord Surya and His unwavering support for sincere devotees. It conveys that anyone embarking on a journey—whether physical, emotional, or spiritual—should listen to or recite the sacred Purana of Surya Dev. Doing so invites auspiciousness, protection, and the successful fulfilment of one's goals.

The chapter particularly emphasizes how Lord Surya's grace can alleviate financial burdens. Those overwhelmed by debt or material struggles are encouraged to embrace this sacred narrative with devotion and faith. Through this, not only are their troubles eased, but wealth and prosperity are also restored. The divine energy of Surya is portrayed as a force that uplifts, heals, and grants all heartfelt desires.

Ultimately, the chapter reassures readers that Lord Surya responds generously to sincere remembrance and recitation of His glories. The power of His light dispels obstacles and paves the way for inner peace and external success, making this chapter a beacon of hope for the devoted.

Fulfilment of all Desires

Surya's Blessings for the Traveler and the Troubled

यात्रा जो नर करै बिदेशा ।
सो नित सुनै पुरान सुरेशा ॥
निश्चय तासु सकल शुभ होई ।
लाभ भवन चलि आवै सोई ॥
जौं चिन्तित रहै ऋण अधिकारी ।
सो यह कथा करे अनुसारी ॥
निश्चय ऋणहु सकल मिट जाई ।
धनि महिमा है सूर्य गोसाँई ॥

Yātrā jo nar karai bideśā,
So nit sunai purān sureśā.
Niśchay tāsu sakal śubh hoī,
Lābh bhavan chali āvai soī.
Jauṁ cintit rahai ṛṇa adhikārī,
So yah kathā kare anusārī.
Niśchay ṛṇahu sakal miṭ jāī,
Dhani mahimā hai Sūrya gosāīṁ.

He who travels to distant lands,
Should daily listen to the
Purana of Lord Surya.
Surely, all good fortune will
come his way,
And wealth will return to his
home.
If one remains anxious due to
debt or financial burden,
Let him follow this sacred tale.
Surely, all his debts will be
wiped away—
Such is the divine glory of Lord
Surya!

दो०- यात्रा को नर जब चले, तब यह सुने पुरान ।
निश्चय मनवांछित सकल, पुरवहिं श्री भगवान ॥
Doha (Couplet):
Yātrā ko nar jab chale, tab yah sune purān,
Niśchay manavānchhit sakal, puravahi Śrī Bhagavān.

When a person sets out on a journey, let him listen to this Purana.
Surely, Lord Surya will fulfil all his heartfelt desires.

इति श्रीमहासूर्य मनवांछित दातानाम चतुर्थोऽध्यायः ॥
Iti Śrīmahāsūrya Manavāñchita Dātānāma Chaturtho'dhyāyaḥ.

Thus ends the fourth chapter titled *"The Granter of Desires—Great Surya."*

CHAPTER 5
THE SAGE'S CURSE AND REDEMPTION

(Aparādhaśāp Nāma Pañchamo'dhyāyaḥ)
– Narad's error, his curse, and Surya's justice.

This chapter from the *Surya Puran* presents a deeply moral tale illustrating the sanctity of devotion and the consequences of transgression, even for the wise. It begins with praise for Lord Surya (Aditya), whose radiant presence removes doubt and bestows bliss upon the faithful. The story unfolds in Simhaldwip, where a devout young maiden worships Surya with unwavering dedication.

During a sacred bath in the Ganges, Sage Narad is momentarily overcome by desire and acts improperly by lifting the maiden's garment from the riverbank. Despite her pleading reminders of dharma, he momentarily falters. Witnessing this, Lord Surya intervenes and, upholding justice, curses the sage for his misconduct.

Humbled and repentant, Narad seeks forgiveness. Lord Shiva, accompanied by Parvati, also appears, and a divine dialogue follows. The chapter ends with Narad accepting the consequences of his actions and praising Surya's mercy, highlighting that divine justice is impartial and that sincere repentance can lead to spiritual redemption.

The Atonement of Sage Narad

ऐसी महिमा आदित देवा ।
करहिं जासु सुर नर मुनि सेवा ॥
मिटै गाढ़ निश्चय मन तासू ।
पुलकित प्रेम मन हरष हुलासू ॥
Aisi mahima Adit Deva,
Karahi jaasu sur nar muni seva.
Mitai gaadh nishchay man taasu,
Pulkit prem man harash hulaasu.

Such is the glory of Lord Aditya (Surya Deva),
Whom gods, humans, and sages serve with devotion.
Deep-rooted doubts in the mind are dispelled,
And the heart rejoices with love, bliss, and divine thrill.

दीनानाथ निरंजन साँई ।
महिमा जाकर बरनि न जाई ॥
सूर्य-कथा मैं कहौं बखानी ।
मन स्थिर करि सुनहु भवानी ॥
Deenanath Niranjan Saai,
Mahima jaakar barani na jaai.
Surya-katha main kahau bakhaani,
Man sthir kari sunahu Bhavani.

He is the Lord of the humble, the pure and ever-radiant one,
Whose glory cannot be fully described.
Now I narrate the divine tale of Surya—
O Bhavani, listen with a calm and steady mind.

करै दंडवत अरु व्रत ध्याना ।
सो तन ले यहि कथा समाना ॥
तेज प्रताप बरनि नहिं जाई ।
सूर्य चरित्र सुनहु मन लाई ॥
Karai dandavat aru vrat dhyana,
So tan le yahi katha samaana.
Tej prataap barani nahin jaai,
Surya charitra sunahu man laai.

One who bows in reverence, observes vows, and meditates,
Should fully embrace this sacred tale within their being.
The brilliance and power of Surya cannot be fully described—
So listen with devotion to the glorious deeds of the Sun!

कहौं सुभग यह कथा पुनीता ।
रवि प्रताप मैं भयउ अजीता ।।
Kahau subhaga yah katha puneeta,
Ravi prataap main bhayau ajeeta.

Let me narrate this blessed and auspicious tale,
By the grace of Surya's glory, I have become victorious and fearless.

दो०- जो महिमा आदित्य की, बरनै प्रेम उछाह ।
सुनहु उमा अति पुलकि तन, कीरति प्रभु अवगाह ॥
Doha (Couplet):
Jo mahima Aditya ki, baranai prem uchchaah.
Sunahu Uma ati pulakit tan, keerati Prabhu avagaah.

He who joyfully sings the glory of Lord Aditya with love,
Listen, O Uma—his whole being is thrilled as he immerses in the Lord's praise.

कहौं पुनीत कथा शुभ बानी ।
बहुरि महातम सुनहु भवानी ॥
कार्तिक चैत पुनीत दिन भारी ।
साजहु अरघ सकल नर-नारी ॥
Kahau puneet katha shubh baani,
Bahuri mahatam sunahu Bhavani.
Kartik Chait puneet din bhaari,
Saajahu argh sakal nar-naari.

I now speak the sacred tale,
filled with auspicious words—
Listen again to its greatness, O Bhavani.
On the holy days of Kartik and Chaitra,
Men and women alike should prepare offerings (Arghya) with devotion.

चन्दन अगर कपूर की बाती ।
पूजा भक्ति करै बहु भाँती ॥
मनोकामना जो मन राखै ।
पुलकित होइ भानु गुन भाखै ॥
Chandan agar kapoor ki baati,
Pooja bhakti karai bahu bhaanti.
Manokamana jo man raakhai,
Pulkit hoi Bhanu gun bhaakhai.

With sandalwood, agarwood,
and camphor wicks,
They should worship the Sun in many devotional ways.
One who holds a wish in their heart,
Should joyfully chant the glories of Bhanu (Surya).

तेहि कल्याण करें भगवाना ।
तेजपुंज प्रभु कृपानिधाना ॥
Tehi kalyaan karen Bhagwana,
Tej-punj Prabhu kripaanidhaana.

The Lord, a reservoir of
compassion and radiance,
Will surely bless such a devotee
with well-being and fulfilment.

दो०- लीला अगम अपार प्रभु, कृपासिंधु भगवान ।
बरनौं कथा पुनीत यह, मन स्थिर करि ध्यान ॥
Doha (Couplet):
Leela agam apaar Prabhu, kripaa-sindhu Bhagwaan.
Baranau katha puneet yah, man sthir kari dhyaan.

The Lord's divine play is unfathomable and infinite; He is the ocean of mercy.
Let me now narrate this sacred tale—focus your mind and listen with deep attention.

सुनहु उमा यह चरित अपारा ।
भानु महातम बहु बिस्तारा ॥
Sunahu Uma yah charit apaara,
Bhanu mahatam bahu bistara.

Listen, O Uma, to this infinite tale—
The greatness of Bhanu (the Sun God) is vast and boundless.

सिंहलद्वीप नगर एक नाँऊ ।
तहाँ निवास परीक्षित राऊ ।
Simhaldweep nagar ek naaun,
Tahaaan nivaas Parikshit raaun.

There was a city named Simhaldwip (Island of Lanka),
Where King Parikshit once resided.

तहाँ पुनीत धर्म नर-नारी ।
तासु भवन एक सुता कुमारी ॥
Tahaaan puneet dharm nar-naari,
Taasu bhavan ek sutaa kumaari.

The men and women there were virtuous and pious,
And in the king's house was a noble young daughter.

सो नित करै भानु की पूजा ।
सेवै सूर्य और नहिं दूजा ॥
So nit karai Bhanu ki pooja,
Sevai Surya aur nahin dooja.

Each day she worshipped Lord Bhanu (the Sun),
She served none other than Surya as her sole deity.

श्रद्धा नेम कथा मन लाई ।
करै हर्ष सो शुभ दिन राई ॥
Shraddha nem katha man laai,
Karai harsh so shubh din raai.

With full faith and disciplined devotion, she focused her mind on Surya's stories,
And joyfully celebrated each auspicious day.

तासु भवन प्रभु करैं कलेवा ।
तीन लोक नहिं जाने मेवा ॥
Taasu bhavan Prabhu karain kaleva,
Teen lok nahin jaane meva.

The Lord (Surya) would accept offerings at her home,
Offerings so divine that even the three worlds could not comprehend their richness.

एक समय अति अचरज भयऊ ।
सुरसरि तीर गमन तेहि ठयऊ ॥
Ek samay ati acharaj bhayau,
Sursari teer gaman tehi thayau.

Then one day, something wondrous occurred—
She went to the bank of the holy Ganga (Sursari) for a pilgrimage.

चीर उतारि भूमि पर धरेऊ ।
कन्या पग जल भीतर करेऊ ॥
Chir utaari bhumi par dhareu,
Kanyā pag jal bhītar kareū.

She placed her clothes on the ground,
And stepped into the water.

मज्जन करन लागि सो बाला ।
हिये बिराजत मोती माला ॥
Majjan karan lāgi so bālā,
Hiye birājat motī mālā.

The maiden had come to bathe,
A pearl necklace adorned her chest.

तेहि अवसर नारद मुनि आये ।
कन्या देखि परम सुख पाये ॥
Tehi avasar Nārad muni āye,
Kanyā dekhi param sukh pāye.

At that very moment, Sage Narad arrived,
And seeing the maiden, he felt great delight.

ठाढ़ भये मुनि सुरसरि तीरा ।
लीन्ह उठाय सुता कर चीरा ॥
Thāṛ bhaye muni Sursari tīrā,
Līnh uthāy sutā kar chīrā.

The sage stood on the bank of the Ganga,
And lifted the girl's garment from the ground.

कन्या जल में करै पुकारी ।
पट दीजै मुनि धर्म बिचारी ॥
Kanyā jal mein karai pukārī,
Pat dījai muni dharm bichārī.

The girl called out from the water,
"O Sage, please return my cloth—think of dharma!"

कह नारद सुनु कन्या बाता ।
मो सँग करहु पुरुष कर नाता ॥
Kah Nārada sunu kanyā bātā,
Mo sang karahu puruṣ kar nātā.

Narad said, "Listen, maiden, to my words—
Join with me in the bond of man and wife."

सुनु मुनि ज्ञानी भये तुम बौरा ।
ऐसे बचन कहौ जनि औरा ॥
Sunu muni jñānī bhaye tum baurā,
Aise bachan kahau jani aurā.

She replied, “Listen, O wise sage,
you have gone astray.
Do not speak such words, which
are unworthy of you.”

अस बानी कस कहेउ मुनीसा ।
हम सन कन्या लाख पचीसा ॥
विनती मोर सुनहु मन बानी ।
देहु बसन तुम मुनि विज्ञानी ॥
As bānī kas kaheū munīsā,
Ham san kanyā lākh pachīsā.
Vinati mor sunahu man bānī,
Dehu basan tum muni vijñānī.

“How could you speak such
words, O revered sage?
I am but a young girl, barely
thirteen years of age.
Please hear my humble plea
with a calm mind—
O wise sage, return my clothes.”

दो०- नग्न नारि जल में खड़ी, कह
मुनिसन करजोरि ।
कृपासिंधु ज्ञाता धरम, अम्बर दीजै मोरि
॥
Doha (Couplet):
Nagn nāri jal meṁ khaṛī, kah
munisan kar jori.
Kripāsindhu jñātā dharam, ambar
dījai mori.

A naked girl stood in the water,
hands folded to the sage,
“O ocean of compassion and
knower of dharma, please give
me back my garment.”

जब कन्या बहु विनती लाई ।
तेहि छन नारद रहे लजाई ॥
अम्बर दे मुनि भवन सिधाये ।
तहँ तबहीं श्री दिनकर आये ॥
Jab kanyā bahu vinati lāī,
Tehi chhan Nārad rahe lajāī.
Ambar de muni bhavan sidhāye,
Tahaṁ tabahīṁ Shri Dinkar āye.

When the girl pleaded repeatedly,
Sage Narad was filled with shame at that moment.
He returned her garment and departed for his ashram,
Just then, Lord Surya (the Sun) arrived there.

सो सुनि मुनिहिं शापबस कीन्हा ।
सो आदित से कहबे लीन्हा ॥
जहँ मैं करत रही असनाना ।
अम्बर ले गये मुनि विज्ञाना ॥
So suni munihīn shāpbasa kīnhā,
So Ādit se kahabe līnhā.
Jahaṁ maiṁ karat rahī asanānā,
Ambar le gaye muni vijñānā.

Hearing this, the girl—under the effect of a curse—spoke it to the Sun:
"I told Aditya what had happened—
As I was bathing, the wise sage took my garment."

ताहीं छन शिव तहाँ सिधारे ।
गौर बदन संग गिरिजा धारे ॥
Tāhīṁ chhan Shiv tahāṁ sidhāre,
Gaur badan sang Girijā dhāre.

At that very moment, Lord Shiva arrived there,
With fair-faced Parvati (Girija) by his side.

भक्ति सहित प्रभु नाये माथा ।
हर्षि शम्भु देखा मुनिनाथा ॥
Bhakti sahit Prabhu nāye māthā,
Harṣi Śhambhu dekhā munināthā.

With devotion, Lord Surya bowed His head,
Shiva was pleased to see the revered sage (Narad).

कुशल कहा मुनि शिव मुसकाई ।
बैठन कहि सब कथा बुझाई ॥
Kushal kahā muni Shiv musakāī,
Baithan kahi sab kathā bujhāī.

Shiva greeted the sage warmly with a smile,
Asked him to sit, and listened to the entire story.

पूछा प्रभु तब शिव करजोरी ।
नाथ सुनहु यह विनती मोरी ॥
Pūchhā Prabhu tab Shiv karjorī,
Nāth sunahu yah vinatī morī.

Then Lord Surya, with folded hands, humbly said to Shiva:
"O Lord, please listen to this request of mine."

यह अपराध कीन्ह मुनि भारी ।
सो अब मोसन कहहु बिचारी ॥
Yah aparādh kīnh muni bhārī,
So ab mosan kahahu bichārī.

"This sage has committed a serious offense,
Now kindly tell me—what punishment should I give him?"

तब प्रभु कहा सुनहु हो भोरा ।
यह कन्या सेवक है मोरा ॥
Tab Prabhu kahā sunahu ho bhorā,
Yah kanyā sevak hai morā.

Then Lord Surya said, "Listen, O innocent one,
This girl is My devotee and servant."

सुनहु हिये धरि के मुनि ज्ञानी ।
किये कुदृष्टि कुधर्म न जानी ॥
Sunahu hiye dhari ke muni jñānī,
Kiye kudṛiṣṭi, kudharm na jānī.

"Understand this well, O learned sage—
You acted with evil intent, ignoring the path of righteousness."

कारन सोइ शाप अब दयऊ ।
तुरतै अंग बरन मुनि लयऊ ॥
Kāran soī shāp ab dayau,
Turatai ang baran muni layau.

"For this reason, I have now
placed a curse upon you—
And instantly, the sage lost the
colour and purity of his body."

इतना कहि दिनकर मुसकाना ।
ज्ञानहीन तब मुनि पहिचाना ॥
Itnā kahi Dinkar musakānā,
Jñān-hīn tab muni pahichānā.

Having said this, Lord Surya
smiled,
And in that moment, the sage
realized his ignorance.

बैन सुनत प्रभु क्रोधित भयऊ ।
कन्या संग लै मुनि पहँ गयऊ ॥
Bain sunat Prabhu krodhit bhayau,
Kanyā sang lai muni pahin gayau.

Hearing her words, the Lord
(Surya) became angry,
And took the girl with Him to
confront the sage.

दो०- बचन सुनत क्रोधित भये, क्रोध न
हिये समाय ।
कौतुक कीन्ह अयुक्त तब, मोसन कहहु
बुझाय ॥
Doha (Couplet):
Bachan sunat krodhit bhaye, krodh
na hiye samāy.
Kautuk kīnh ayukt tab, mosan
kahahu bujhāy.

Hearing her words, He grew
furious—anger could not be
contained.
"You acted improperly in play—
now explain this to Me!"

जोरि पाणि मुनि बचन सुनाये ।
धरि पद-कमल सूर्य-गुण गाये ॥
Jori pāṇi muni bachan sunāye,
Dhari pad-kamal Sūrya-guṇ gāye.

With folded hands, the sage spoke humbly,
And praised Surya's lotus feet and divine virtues.

कह मुनि सुनु प्रभु बचन हमारी ।
भा मोसन अपराध है भारी ॥
यह अपराध क्षमा प्रभु कीजै ।
दीनानाथ अनुग्रह दीजै ॥
Kah muni sunu Prabhu bachan hamārī,
Bhā mosan aparādh hai bhārī.
Yah aparādh kṣhamā Prabhu kījai,
Dīnānāth anugrah dījai.

The sage said, "O Lord, please listen to my words—
I have indeed committed a grave offense.
O Compassionate Lord of the humble, please forgive me,
And bestow Your grace upon me."

तब प्रभु कहा सुनहु मम बानी ।
उतर के लोग सकल अज्ञानी ॥
तेहि अपराध लेहु मुनि शापा ।
जस कीन्हेउ तस भोगहु पापा ॥
Tab Prabhu kahā sunu mam bānī,
Uttar ke log sakal ajñānī.
Tehi aparādh lehu muni shāpā,
Jas kīnheu tas bhogahu pāpā.

Then the Lord said, "Listen to My words—
People of the North are ignorant and unaware.
For this offense, accept this curse, O Sage—
As you have done, so shall you now bear the consequences of your sin."

दो०- त्रिभुवन स्वामी मोहि पर, करहु ज्योति परकास ।
हर्षित गावहिं गुण विमल, कहाँ मोर भव बास ॥
Doha (Couplet):
Tribhuvan Swāmī mohi par, karahu jyoti prakās.
Harṣit gāvahi guṇ vimal, kahāṁ mor bhav bās.

O Lord of the Three Worlds,
shine Your light upon me.
Let me sing Your pure glories with joy—
Where then is the place for worldly suffering in my life?

इति श्रीसूर्यपुराण अपराध-शापोनाम पंचमोऽध्यायः ॥
Iti Shri Suryapuran aparādh-shāponāma panchamo'dhyāyah.

Thus ends the fifth chapter of the Surya Puran,
Titled *"The Curse for the Offense."*

CHAPTER 6
THE SUN'S MAJESTIC JOURNEY

(Mahā-Astāchal Varṇana Nāma Ṣaṣṭho'dhyāyaḥ)
– Description of Surya's journey from east to west.

Chapter 6 unfolds a captivating description of Lord Surya's divine journey across the heavens—from His rising in the east to His setting in the west (Astācala). The chapter celebrates Surya's majestic radiance as He traverses the skies, illuminating all three worlds and bestowing vitality upon creation. Each moment of this celestial movement is imbued with spiritual symbolism and cosmic significance.

As Lord Shiva narrates the tale to Goddess Parvati, the focus turns toward the sacred geography and the places blessed by Surya's presence—especially in the southern direction. The city of Pampa (modern-day Hampi or its surroundings) and various spiritual locations emerge as luminous centers of devotion where sages, deities, and righteous kings worship Surya with faith and rituals.

This chapter also emphasizes the power of observing Sunday fasts, chanting Surya's names, and living a dharmic life. Through these practices, devotees earn the Lord's grace, spiritual clarity, and freedom from suffering. It underscores that Surya is not just a celestial body but the eternal witness, inner light, and remover of darkness—both within and without.

Ultimately, Chapter 6 inspires seekers to turn toward Surya with reverence, observe spiritual discipline, and walk the path of truth, which leads to divine blessings, purification, and inner illumination.

The Path of Devotion and the Southern Pilgrimage

पम्पापुर एक नगर को नाऊँ ।
हलधर विप्र तहाँ एक राऊ ॥
Pampāpur ek nagar ko nāūṁ,
Haladhar vipra tahāṁ ek rāūṁ.

There was a city named Pampapur,
Where a Brahmin named Haladhar lived as a noble and respected man.

नगर बसै मानो कैलाशा ।
धर्म-कथा तहँ होइ प्रकाशा ॥
Nagar basai māno Kailāshā,
Dharma-kathā tahāṁ hoi prakāshā.

The city appeared as divine as Mount Kailash itself,
Where discourses on dharma and sacred tales were constantly shared.

पूजन करै भानु दिन-राती ।
निशि दिन टेक धरै बहु भाँती ॥
Pūjan karai Bhānu din-rātī,
Nishi din ṭek dharai bahu bhāṁtī.

He worshipped Lord Surya, day and night,
Holding firm devotion in various ways, without fail.

कोटि अग्नि चारिहुँ दिशि माहीं ।
श्री सूर्य को आश्रम ताहीं ॥
Koṭi agni chārihuṁ disi māhīṁ,
Shri Sūrya ko āshram tāhīṁ.

The radiance of a million fires shone in all directions,
For that place was the divine hermitage of Lord Surya.

रतन जड़ित सर तहाँ सुहावा ।
कनक घाट चहुँ ओर बनावा ॥
Ratan jaḍit sar tahāṁ suhāvā,
Kanak ghāṭ chahuṁ or banāvā.

A beautiful lake, studded with precious gems, was there,
With golden banks crafted all around.

यहाँ खम्भ एक परम बिसाला ।
शत योजन सो उच्च रसाला ॥
Yahāṁ khambh ek param bisālā,
Shat yojan so uchch rasālā.

There stood a grand and massive pillar,
One hundred yojanas* (over 700 miles) tall and majestic.

तेहि खम्भा आदित कर बासा ।
जात खम्भ सो लाग अकाशा ॥
Tehi khambhā Ādit kar bāsā,
Jāt khambh so lāg ākāshā.

On that very pillar resided the Sun God (Aditya),
The pillar reached so high that it seemed to touch the sky.

योजन लक्ष सो उदय कराहीं ।
योजन सहस एक पल जाहीं ॥
Yojan lakṣa so uday karāhīṁ,
Yojan sahas ek pal jāhīṁ.

The Sun rises a hundred thousand yojanas in the sky,
And travels a thousand yojanas in just one moment.

प्रात होत उदयाचल बासा ।
अस्ताचल पर करहिं निबासा ॥
Prāt hot Udayāchal bāsā,
Astāchal par karahiṁ nibāsā.

At dawn, He (the Sun) resides on Mount Udayachal (the eastern mountain),
And at dusk, He sets behind Mount Astachal (the western mountain).

* *1 yojana ≈ 8 to 15 kilometres, depending on the historical text or region. It was commonly used in Vedic and Puranic scriptures to describe distances—especially in cosmic or mythological contexts.*

यहि विधि आदित आवहिं जाहीं ।
समुझ पुनीत कथा मन माहीं ॥
Yahi vidhi Ādit āvahiṁ jāhīṁ,
Samujh puneet kathā man māhīṁ.

In this way, Aditya (the Sun) rises and sets daily—
Understand this sacred story and keep it in your heart.

आदित कथा सुनहु मन लाई ।
मैं तोहि अर्थ कहौं समुझाई ॥
Ādit kathā sunahu man lāī,
Main tohi arth kahau samujhāī.

Listen attentively to the tale of Aditya (Surya),
I will now explain its meaning to you with clarity.

दो०- धन्य भानु ईश्वर प्रभु, महिमा अगम अपार ।
तीन लोक छवि ज्योतिमय, है जाकर उजियार ॥
Doha (Couplet):
Dhanya Bhānu Īśwar Prabhu, mahimā agam apār.
Tīn lok chhavi jyotimay, hai jākār ujiyār.

Blessed is Bhanu (Surya), the Lord and Supreme God,
Whose infinite and unfathomable glory illuminates all three worlds.

कुष्ठी ध्यावै भक्ति कर, पावै काया दान ।
अन्तर्यामी दयानिधि, कृपा करहिं भगवान ॥
Kuṣṭhī dhyāvai bhakti kar, pāvai kāyā dān.
Antaryamı dayanıdhı, kṛipa karahim Bhagwān.

Even a leper, if he meditates upon Him with devotion, will be gifted a healthy body.
The Lord, knower of all hearts and ocean of mercy, bestows His grace.

सुरनर मुनि अस्तुति करहिं, हौं प्रसन्न भगवान ।
जो नित मन व्रत करै, श्रद्धा प्रीति समान ॥
Surnar muni astuti karahiṁ, haun prasann Bhagwān.
Jo nit man vrat karai, śraddhā prīti samān.

Gods and sages praise Him constantly, and the Lord is pleased—
Especially with one who daily observes vows with faith and love.

सब गुण आगर बुद्धि वर, सुन्दर शीलनिधान ।
मन वच कर्म हर्षयुत, जो नर करहि बखान ॥
Sab guṇ āgar buddhi var, sundar śīl-nidhān.
Man-vach-karma harṣayut, jo nar karahiṁ bakhān.

He is the source of all virtues, endowed with supreme intellect, and a treasure of noble character.
Whoever praises Him with joy—in mind, speech, and deed—receives His divine favour.

॥ इति श्रीसूर्यमहाअस्ताचलवर्णनोनाम षष्ठोऽध्यायः ॥
Iti Shri Sūrya Mahā-Astachalvarṇanonāma Ṣhaṣṭho'dhyāyaḥ.

Thus ends the sixth chapter titled *"The Great Description of the Setting Sun"* in the Surya Puran.

CHAPTER 7
THE EASTERN DAWN OF DHARMA

(Pūrvottara Udaya Varṇana Nāma Saptamo'dhyāyaḥ)
– Where and how Surya rises; geography and metaphysics.

This chapter explores the mystical emergence of Surya in the eastern direction, known as *Pūrva Disha*, and the profound significance of His daily rising. Lord Shiva narrates to Goddess Parvati the awe-inspiring journey of the Sun God, emphasizing how His ascent dispels ignorance, awakens wisdom, and rejuvenates all life forms.

The chapter paints vivid images of divine cities and majestic mountains in the east where Surya's presence is most potent. Among them is a sacred mountain where the Sun God dwells and from where His radiance spreads across the universe. The narrative illustrates how sages, kings, and celestial beings worship Surya at dawn, recognizing it as a time of spiritual awakening and supreme clarity.

It also praises Surya as the giver of joy, intellect, health, and righteousness. The rituals, prayers, and disciplines performed at sunrise are described as especially effective, purifying both body and soul. The power of chanting Surya's names and listening to His glories at dawn is portrayed as a gateway to liberation.

Ultimately, Chapter 7 highlights the east not merely as a direction but as a spiritual metaphor for enlightenment, with Surya's rise symbolizing the beginning of transformation, devotion, and divine realization.

The Dawn in the Eastern Skies

गिरिजा कह्यो सो कहौं गुसाँई ।
सो मोहिं अर्थ कहौ समुझाई ॥
Girijā kahyo so kahau gusāī,
So mohiṁ arth kahau samujhāī.

Then Girija (Parvati) spoke: "O Lord,
Please explain to me the meaning behind what You have said."

कहन लगे शिव, कथा रसाला ।
जेहि विधि ऊगहिं पूर्व कृपाला ॥
Kahan lage Shiv, kathā rasālā,
Jehi vidhi ūgahiṁ pūrv kṛipālā.

Shiva then began to speak the sweet tale,
Explaining how the merciful Lord (Surya) rises in the east.

गिरिजा सुनहु कथा मन लाई ।
मैं तोहिं अर्थ कहौं समुझाई ॥
Girijā sunahu kathā man lāī,
Main tohiṁ arth kahauṁ samujhāī.

Listen, O Girija (Parvati), with full attention to this sacred tale—
I will now explain its meaning clearly to you.

पूर्व दिशा एक श्रीपुर देशा ।
तहँ के राजा रूप महेशा ॥
Pūrv dishā ek Shrīpur deshā,
Tahaṁ ke rājā rūp maheśā.

In the eastern direction, there is a land named Shripur,
Ruled by a king of great beauty and noble form.

सदा करै आदित की पूजा ।
सेवै सूर्य और नहिं दूजा ॥
Sadā karai Ādit kī pūjā,
Sevai Sūrya aur nahin dūjā.

He always worshipped the Sun (Aditya),
And served no other deity except Surya.

यहि विधि सकल नगर उजियारा ।
तहाँ एक गिरि अगम अपारा ॥
Yahi vidhi sakal nagar ujiyārā,
Tahaṁ ek giri agam apārā.

Because of this devotion, the whole city was filled with light,
And there stood a vast, unfathomable mountain nearby.

सहस कोस पर्वत परमाना ।
बसै तहाँ आदित बलवाना ॥
Sahas kos parvat paramānā,
Basai tahaṁ Ādit balavānā.

That mountain stretched for thousands of kos (ancient miles),
And there resided the mighty Lord Aditya (Sun God).

उगै जाहिं तहँ करे निबासा ।
पुनि पश्चिम दिशि करहिं प्रकासा ॥
Ugai jāhiṁ tahaṁ kare nibāsā,
Puni paścim dishi karahiṁ prakāsā.

He (Surya) rose from there and made it His dwelling,
Then travelled westward to shine His light upon the world.

मन वच कर्म कथा वर गाई ।
सूर्य चरित विधि तुमहिं सुनाई ॥
Man-vach-karma kathā var gāī,
Sūrya charit vidhi tumhiṁ sunāī.

With mind, speech, and action, I have narrated this great tale—
Thus have I shared with you the glorious deeds of Surya as ordained by divine law.

सुनि गिरिजा सुन्दर यह बानी ।
बल प्रताप सुनि मन हरषानी ॥
Suni Girijā sundar yah bānī,
Bal pratāp suni man haraṣānī.

Hearing these beautiful words,
O Girija (Parvati),
You were delighted by the
power and glory of the Sun.

धन्य भानु जिनकी यह लीला ।
धर्म धुरन्धर परम सुशीला ॥
Dhanya Bhānu jinakī yah līlā,
Dharm dhurandhar param suśīlā.

Blessed is Lord Bhanu (Surya),
whose divine acts are glorious—
He is the upholder of dharma
and the embodiment of
supreme virtue.

जो नर कथा सूर्य की गावै ।
चढ़ि विमान बैकुण्ठ सिधावै ॥
Jo nar kathā Sūrya kī gāvai,
Charhi vimān Baikuṇṭh sidhāvai.

Whoever sings the tale of Lord
Surya,
Ascends a celestial chariot and
reaches Vaikuntha (the eternal
abode).

सूर्य चरित सुनि अमृत बानी ।
अस्तुति हर्षित करैं भवानी ॥
Sūrya charit suni amrit bānī,
Astituti harṣit karaiṁ Bhavānī.

Upon hearing the nectar-like
story of Surya,
Even Goddess Bhavani (Parvati)
rejoices and offers praise.

हे जगस्वामी अन्तर्यामी, ज्योतिकला
छवि उदित महा ।
गुणातीत निधाना श्रीभगवाना, करे कृपा
हे धर्म महा ॥
Hymn to Surya:
He Jaga-swāmī antar-yāmī, jyoti-
kalā chhavi udit mahā,
Guṇātīt nidhānā Shrībhagwānā,
kare kṛipā he dharm mahā.

O Lord of the universe, knower of all hearts, source of divine light and radiant brilliance,
O Supreme Lord beyond all qualities, bestow Your grace—You are the great sustainer of dharma.

छवि ज्योति बिराजै कुण्डल राज़ै, तव
प्रताप महिमा बरना ।
तव हेतु घनेरा सब प्रभु तेरा, लेत नाम
पातक हरना ॥
Chhavi jyoti birājai, kuṇḍal rājai,
Tav pratāp mahimā barnā.
Tav hetu ghanerā, sab prabhu terā,
Let nām pātak harnā.

Your radiance shines gloriously; Your earrings gleam with splendour,
Your divine power and glory cannot be fully described.
For Your sake, all beings worship—O Lord, Your very name destroys all sins.

दो०- करहु कृपा अब मोहि पर, अति छबि ज्योति बिराज ।
तेज विपुल तिहुँलोक महुँ, जय जय जय महराज ॥
Doha (Couplet):
Karahu kṛipā ab mohi par, ati chhavi jyoti birāj.
Tej vipul tihũlok maṁh, jay jay jay Mahārāj.

Please shower Your grace upon me now, O radiant and resplendent Lord.
Your immense brilliance lights all three worlds—Victory, Victory, Victory to You, O Great King!

इति श्रीमहासूर्यपूर्वपूर्वदिशि उदयोनाम सप्तमोऽध्यायः ॥
Iti Shrī Mahāsūrya Pūrva-pūrvadishi Udayonāma Saptamo'dhyāyaḥ.

Thus ends the seventh chapter titled *"The Great Sunrise in the Far Eastern Direction"* from the Mahā Sūrya Purāṇa.

CHAPTER 8
THE YAJÑA OF ENLIGHTENMENT

(Sūryanārāyaṇa Varṇana Nāma Aṣṭamo'dhyāyaḥ)
– Universal reverence for Surya by all divine beings.

In this vibrant and devotional chapter, the sage Narad Muni organizes a grand yajna (sacred fire ritual) in honour of Lord Surya. The event becomes a cosmic celebration, as invitations are sent across the three worlds, drawing gods, sages, celestial beings, and mortals alike.

The chapter describes the elaborate arrangements made for this holy gathering, highlighting the spiritual and festive atmosphere. Lord Brahma, Vishnu, Shiva (Tripurari), and many others arrive on their divine vehicles. Vedic chants, hymns, and offerings fill the air, glorifying the Sun God as the source of light, life, and righteousness.

Women sing auspicious songs, sages recite Vedic mantras, and aromatic flowers, ghee, and sandalwood perfume the space. The sacrificial fire becomes the centre of divine communion and universal harmony. Narad's devotion, combined with meticulous ritual conduct, pleases Surya immensely.

This chapter emphasizes that sincere devotion and collective reverence toward Surya bring harmony, blessings, and the destruction of cosmic and individual darkness. It serves as a reminder that honouring Surya through yajna and unity can elevate entire societies toward spiritual well-being and divine grace.

The Divine Gathering and Yajna of Narad Muni

उत्तर दिशि कहँ उगहिं गोसाँई । मैं तोहिं अर्थ कहौं समुझाई ॥ Uttar dishi kahāṁ ugahiṁ Gosāī, Main tohiṁ arth kahauṁ samujhāī.	Now I shall tell you how the Lord rises in the northern direction, And explain its meaning to you clearly.
उत्तर दिशि एक नगर विशाला । राज करैं तहँ मदन गोपाला ॥ Uttar dishi ek nagar vishālā, Rāj karaiṁ tahaṁ Madan Gopālā.	In the northern direction, there was a vast city, Where a king named Madan Gopala ruled.
तहाँ शैल एक परम विशाला । शत योजन परमान कराला ॥ Tahaṁ shail ek param vishālā, Shat yojan parmān karālā.	There stood a mighty mountain nearby, Measuring a hundred yojanas in height—enormous and terrifying.
तापर भानु किरन नहिं जावै । यहि विधि पुर अँधियार जनावै ॥ Tāpar Bhānu kiran nahin jāvai, Yahi vidhi pur andhiār janāvai.	Sunlight could not reach beyond that mountain, Thus, the entire city remained shrouded in darkness.

निशा घोर सब पुर अँधियारी ।
उगै न रवि न होइ उजियारी ॥
Nishā ghor sab pur andhiārī,
Ugai na Ravi, na hoi ujiyārī.

The night was deep and all-encompassing in that city,
The Sun never rose there, and no light ever reached.

तहाँ बास कलियुग कर होई ।
परम मलेच्छ बसत तहँ सोई ।
Tahaṁ bās Kaliyug kar hoī,
Param malechchh basat tahaṁ soī.

It became the dwelling place of the dark age—Kaliyug,
Filled with impure and unrighteous beings (Mlechchhas).

यहि कारन तहँ उगै न भानू ।
मैं तोहि कथा कहौं परमानू ॥
Yahi kāran tahaṁ ugai na Bhānū,
Main tohiṁ kathā kahauṁ paramānū.

For this reason, the Sun does not rise there,
And now I shall tell you the full story behind it.

एक समय अचरज अति भयऊ ।
नारद मुनि तहाँ चलि गयऊ ।।
Ek samay acharaj ati bhayau,
Nārad muni tahaṁ chali gayau.

Once, a great and wondrous event occurred—
Sage Narad travelled to that very place.

देखा नगर सकल अँधियारा ।
धर्म-कथा कर कहुँ न प्रचारा ॥
Dekha nagar sakal andhiārā,
Dharma-kathā kar kahuṁ na prachārā.

Narad saw that the entire city was engulfed in darkness,
And there was no discourse or spread of dharma or sacred stories.

फिरि-फिरि सकल नगर मुनि देखा ।
अघ ब्योहार अपर नहिं लेखा ॥
Phiri-phiri sakal nagar muni dekhā,
Agh vyavahār apar nahiṁ lekhā.

He wandered through the city again and again,
And found nothing but sinful conduct and unrighteous ways.

मन महँ नारद कीन्ह बिचारा ।
कहँ आये यहि पुर अँधियारा ॥
Man maṁh Nārad kīnh bichārā,
Kahāṁ āye yahi pur andhiārā?

Narad pondered in his heart,
"What kind of dark and impure city have I come to?"

अस कहि नारद कोपेउ जबहीं ।
दीन्हा शाप नगर कहँ तबहीं ॥
As kahi Nārad kopeyau jabahīṁ,
Dīnhā śāp nagar kahuṁ tabahīṁ.

Saying this, Narad grew angry,
And at once placed a curse upon the entire city.

कुष्ठी होउ सकल नर-नारी ।
धर्म-कथा कर नाम बिसारी ॥
Kuṣṭhī hoū sakal nar-nārī,
Dharma-kathā kar nām bisārī.

"Let all men and women be afflicted with leprosy,
For they have forgotten the name and stories of dharma."

कुष्ठ बरन भा सबके अंगा । आठो गात कुष्ठ तन भंगा ॥ Kuṣṭh baran bhā sabke aṅgā, Āṭho gāt kuṣṭh tan bhaṅgā.	Disfigurement covered the skin of everyone, All eight limbs were afflicted by the disease.
रहा न कोऊ कुष्ठ बिहीना । जबहीं शाप मुनीश्वर दीन्हा ॥ Rahā na koū kuṣṭh bihīnā, Jabahīṁ śāp Munīśvar dīnhā.	Not a single person remained free from leprosy, Once the sage (Narad) had pronounced the curse.
ब्याकुल भये सकल नर-नारी । त्राहि-त्राहि सब करहिं पुकारी ॥ Byākul bhaye sakal nar-nārī, Trāhi-trāhi sab karahiṁ pukārī.	All the men and women became restless and desperate, Crying out for help in pain and suffering.
शाप देइ उत्तर पहँ आये । अब हम यह मुनि चरित सुनाये ॥ Śāp dei uttar pahin āye, Ab ham yah muni charit sunāye.	After giving the curse, the sage returned to the north, Now we shall narrate the rest of the sage's story.
अब कह मुनि पूछौं मैं तोही । उग्र शाप कब छूटे मोंही ॥ Ab kah muni pūchhauṁ maiṁ tohi, Ugra śāp kab chhūṭe mohi?	Then the sage asked (the Lord), "O Lord, when will this terrible curse be lifted from me?"

अंग बरन मुनि देखा कैसा । हंस समान श्वेत भा जैसा ॥ Aṅg baran muni dekhā kaisā, Haṁs samān śvet bhā jaisā.	The appearance of the sage's body became transformed, His complexion turned white and pure like a swan.
बिदा होइ मुनिवर घर आये । हर्षित होइ भानु गुण गाये ।। Bidā ho'i munivar ghar āye, Harṣit ho'i Bhānu guṇ gāye.	Taking leave, the great sage returned to his abode, Filled with joy, singing the praises of Lord Bhanu (Surya).
धनि आदित काया के राजा । ज्योति जासु तिहुँलोक बिराजा ॥ Dhani Ādit kāyā ke rājā, Jyoti jāsu tihūṁlok birājā.	Blessed is Aditya, the sovereign of the physical body, Whose light illuminates all the three worlds.
अस्तुति रवि कर नारद गाये । कोटि विप्र तहँ नेवत पठाये ॥ Astituti Ravi kar Nārad gāye, Koṭi vipra tahuṁ nevata pathāye.	Narad sang hymns in praise of Ravi (Surya), And sent invitations to a crore (ten million) Brahmins.
भोजन सुधा समान बनाये । प्रेम सहित सब विप्र जिमाये ॥ Bhojan sudhā samān banāye, Prem sahit sab vipra jimāye.	He prepared food as divine as nectar, And lovingly served all the Brahmins.

अश्वमेध मुनि करने सो लागे ।
तीन लोक के दारिद भागे ॥
Aśvamedh muni karne so lāge,
Tīn lok ke dārid bhāge.

Then the sage began the Ashvamedha sacrifice,
And poverty fled from all three worlds.

सब कहँ नारद नेवत पठाये ।
निज-निज वाहन चढ़ि-चढ़ि आये ॥
Sab kahṁ Nārad nevat pathāye,
Nij-nij vāhan chaṛhi-chaṛhi āye.

Narad sent invitations to all,
And everyone arrived riding their respective vehicles.

ब्रह्मा विष्णु और त्रिपुरारी ।
आए सहित सबै नर-नारी ॥
Brahmā, Viṣṇu aur Tripurārī,
Āye sahit sabai nar-nārī.

Brahma, Vishnu, and Shiva (Tripurari) came,
Accompanied by countless men and women.

बहु प्रकार मुनि सबहिं जेंवाए ।
हरषित होय भानु गुन गाए ॥
Bahu prakār muni sabahiṁ jemvāye,
Harṣit hoy Bhānu guṇ gāye.

The sage offered a grand feast to all in many ways,
And with great joy, they all sang the glories of Surya (Bhanu).

वेद पढ़ें मुनि गिरा उचारी ।
हरषित गावहिं मंगल नारी ॥
Ved paṛheṁ muni girā uchārī,
Harṣit gāvahiṁ maṅgal nārī.

The sages recited the Vedas aloud,
While joyful women sang auspicious songs.

चन्दन अक्षत लै पकवाना ।
पूजा करहिं मुनिवर धर ध्याना ॥
Chandan akṣat lai pakvānā,
Pūjā karahiṁ munivar dhar dhyānā.

With sandalwood paste, rice grains, and delicious offerings, The great sage performed worship with deep meditation.

ब्रह्मादिक निज लोक सिधाए ।
प्रेम पुलकि सूरज गुन गाए ॥
Brahmādik nij lok sidhāye,
Prem pulakit Sūraj guṇ gāye.

Then Brahma and the other gods returned to their divine abodes, singing the glories of the Sun with love and bliss in their hearts.

दो०- यज्ञ कीन्ह मुनिवर सविधि, शोभा बरनि न जाय ।
देव कोटि तैंतीस तहँ, हरषि भानु गुन गाय ॥
Doha (Couplet):
Yajña kīnh munivar savidhi, śobhā barani na jāy.
Dev koṭi taintīs tahaṁ, harṣi Bhānu guṇ gāy.

The sage performed the yajña (sacrifice) with perfect ritual—its beauty was beyond description.
All the 33 crore (330 million) deities rejoiced, singing the praises of Bhanu (the Sun God).

इति श्रीसूर्यनारायणवर्णनोनाम अष्टमोऽध्यायः ॥
Iti Shri Sūryanārāyaṇa-varṇanonāma aṣṭamo'dhyāyaḥ.

Thus ends the eighth chapter titled *"The Glorious Description of Lord Sūryanārāyaṇa"* in the Surya Puran.

Chapter 9
Surya and the Age of Darkness

(Dakṣiṇodaya Mahākaliyuga Varṇana Nāma Navamo'dhyāyaḥ) – Surya's role in Kali Yuga and restoring dharma.

Chapter 9 presents a profound prophecy describing the role of Lord Surya in the Kali Yuga, the current and most turbulent of the four ages. As ignorance, falsehood, and unrighteousness spread across the world, Surya emerges as a beacon of spiritual discipline, purity, and redemption.

Shiva reveals to Parvati how, in the darkest times, when virtue declines and people lose moral direction, those who follow the path of Surya devotion will be protected. The Sun will rise in the south, and the faithful will engage in righteous deeds like fasting on Sundays, reciting the *Surya Puran*, feeding Brahmins, applying holy ash, and performing rituals with sincerity.

Surya is described as the destroyer of falsehood and affliction. Even in Kali Yuga, he continues to grant health, clarity, strength, and divine insight to his devotees. The chapter outlines how each lunar month has a unique connection to Surya, and practicing specific observances during these times leads to both worldly and spiritual gains.

This chapter inspires readers to embrace discipline, self-purification, and unwavering faith in Surya, even amid the chaos of the present age. It highlights that divine order and personal upliftment are possible through the consistent light of the Sun.

Surya's Blessings in the Age of Kali

जो नर धरै सूर्य पर ध्याना ।
ताकर होइ पुत्र कल्याना ॥
Jo nar dharai Sūrya par dhyānā,
Tākar hohi putra kalyānā.

Whoever meditates upon Lord Surya,
Will be blessed with virtuous and noble sons.

जो रवि-कथा सुनै मन लाई ।
तापर दिनकर होहिं सहाई ॥
Jo Ravi-kathā sunai man lāī,
Tāpar Dinkar hohiṁ sahāī.

Whoever listens attentively to the tales of Ravi (the Sun),
Lord Dinkar (Surya) becomes their protector and helper.

धर्म प्रताप आदित बलवाना ।
तेज प्रताप है अग्नि समाना ॥
Dharm pratāp Ādit balavānā,
Tej pratāp hai agni samānā.

Aditya (Surya) is mighty with the power of dharma,
His brilliance and strength are like blazing fire.

दो०- पूछत गिरिजा शंभुसन, भानु चरित मनलाय ।
दक्षिण दिशा पुनीत है, नाथ कहौं समुझाय ॥
Doha (Couplet):
Pūchhat Girijā Śambhusan, Bhānu charit manlāy.
Dakṣiṇ dishā puneet hai, Nāth kahauṁ samujhāy.

As Girija (Parvati) asked Lord Shambhu (Shiva) about the Sun's divine deeds,
He replied, "The southern direction is sacred—let Me explain its story."

हे गिरिजा सुनु शैलकुमारी ।
कहिहौं भानु चरित बिस्तारी ॥
He Girijā sunu Śailkumārī,
Kahihauṁ Bhānu charit bistārī.

O Girija, daughter of the mountain, listen well—
I shall now describe in detail the glorious deeds of Lord Bhanu (Surya).

कहन लगे शिव कथा रसाला ।
जेहि विधि दक्षिण उगहिं कृपाला ॥
Kahan lage Shiv kathā rasālā,
Jehi vidhi dakṣiṇ ugahiṁ kṛipālā.

Then Shiva began the delightful tale,
Describing how the compassionate Sun rises in the southern direction.

वर्णन करहिं अर्थ समुझाई ।
सुनहु सत्य गिरिजा मन लाई ॥
Varṇan karahiṁ arth samujhāī,
Sunahu satya Girijā man lāī.

He narrated with meaning and explanation,
"Listen closely, O Girija, to this true and sacred account."

दक्षिण दिशि एक नगर अनूपा ।
जयमल विप्र तहाँ कर भूपा ॥
Dakṣiṇ dishi ek nagar anūpā,
Jayamal vipra tahaṁ kar bhūpā.

In the southern direction, there was a magnificent city,
Where a Brahmin named Jayamal ruled as king.

हर्षित भजन करै दिन-राती ।
तहाँ करै प्रभु सुख बहु भाँती ॥
Harṣit bhajan karai din-rātī,
Tahaṁ karai Prabhu sukh bahu bhāṁtī.

Joyfully, the people sang devotional hymns day and night,
And the Lord (Surya) granted them happiness in many ways.

यहि विधि प्रभु कर ज्योति बिराजै । अनहद नाद घंट धुनि बाजै ॥ Yahi vidhi Prabhu kar jyoti birājai, Anahad nād ghaṇṭ dhuni bājai.	In this way, the divine light of the Lord shone brilliantly, As the sound of celestial bells and unstruck divine melody (anahad nād) resonated.
तैंतीस कोटि देवता जहवाँ । श्री सूर्य कर आश्रम तहवाँ ॥ Taintīs koṭi devatā jahvāṁ, Shrī Sūrya kar āśram tahvāṁ.	There, the thirty-three crore (330 million) gods reside, For that sacred place is the hermitage of Lord Surya.
दक्षिण दिशि काशी परियागा । तहँ के लोग सकल बड़भागा ॥ Dakṣiṇ dishi Kāśī Pariyāgā, Tahaṁ ke log sakal baṛabhāgā.	In the southern direction lie sacred cities like Kashi and Prayag, The people living there are truly most fortunate.
दोउ भलभद्र सहोदर संगा । तहाँ बहैं सरिता बड़ गंगा ॥ Doū Bhalabhadra sahodar saṅgā, Tahaṁ bahaiṁ saritā baṛ Gaṅgā.	There, both Balaram and Krishna (brothers) had once come together, And the mighty river Ganga flows through that holy land.
कृपासिन्धु प्रभु परम अगाधा । निशि दिन सुमिरत नाथ अबाधा ॥ Kṛipasindhu Prabhu param agādhā, Nishi-din sumirat Nāth abādhā.	The Lord is an ocean of mercy, immeasurable and vast, He is remembered day and night without hindrance.

दो०- दक्षिण दिशा पुनीत है, सुनहु उमा मन लाय ।
सुमन अर्थ जैसे अहैं, तैसे कहौं बुझाय ॥
Doha (Couplet):
Dakṣiṇ dishā puneet hai, sunahu Umā man lāy.
Suman arth jaise ahaiṁ, taise kahauṁ bujhāy.

The southern direction is sacred—listen carefully, O Uma,
I shall now explain it to you as sweetly and meaningfully as flowers convey fragrance.

कलि ब्यापित जबहीं है जैहैं ।
मानुष को धरि मानुष खैहैं ॥
Kalī byāpit jabahīṁ hai jaihaiṁ,
Mānuṣ ko dhari mānuṣ khaihaiṁ.

When the age of Kali spreads fully,
Humans will devour other humans, disguised in human form.

तब प्रभु धरि अवतार कलंकी ।
मानुष तन है जैहैं पंखी ।
Tab Prabhu dhari avatar Kalaṅkī,
Mānuṣ tan hai jaihaiṁ paṅkhī.

Then the Lord shall take the Kalki Avatar,
And though in human form,
He will move as swiftly as a bird.

तब दक्षिण दिशि उदय कराहीं ।
आगिल अर्थ कहौं तुम पाहीं ॥
Tab dakṣiṇ dishi uday karāhīṁ,
Āgil arth kahauṁ tum pāhīṁ.

At that time, He will rise in the southern direction,
And now I shall explain the future meaning of this to you.

धर्म-कथा होइहैं दिन-राती ।
नेम धर्म करिहैं बहुभाँती ॥
Dharm-kathā hoihaiṁ din-rātī,
Nema dharm karihaiṁ bahu bhāṁtī.

Religious stories and spiritual discourse will happen day and night,
People will observe discipline and follow dharma in many ways.

विप्र जिमाय के होम करावै ।
वाहि भस्म लै अंग लगावै ॥
Vipra jimāy ke hom karāvai,
Vāhi bhasm lai aṅg lagāvai.

They will feed Brahmins and conduct sacred fire rituals,
Then apply the holy ash from the yajna upon their bodies.

विप्र जेंवाय आप तब खैहैं ।
निशि-दिन कथा सूर्य कर गैहैं ॥
Vipra jemvāy āp tab khaihaiṁ,
Nishi-din kathā Sūrya kar gaihaiṁ.

Only after feeding the Brahmins will they eat themselves,
Day and night they will sing and recite the glories of Surya.

यहि प्रति कमला करहिं निवासा ।
धर्म दया करि होइ प्रकासा ॥
Yahi prati Kamalā karahiṁ nivāsā,
Dharm-dayā kari hohi prakāsā.

Then even Goddess Lakshmi (Kamalā) will dwell there,
And dharma and compassion will shine everywhere.

मिथ्या बचन कोउ ना भाखै ।
धर्म बिचार भानु तप राखै ॥
Mithyā bachan koū nā bhākhai,
Dharm bichār Bhānu tap rākhai.

No one will speak false words,
And the radiance of Bhanu (Surya) will uphold the values of righteousness.

दो०- द्वादश कला उगहिं जब, आदि अन्त तब आय ।
पूर्व जन्म के सकल अघ, कहत सुनत क्षय जाय ॥
Doha (Couplet):
Dvādaś kalā ugahiṁ jab, ādi-ant tab āy.
Pūrv janm ke sakal agh, kahat sunat kṣhay jāy.

When all twelve rays (kalās) of the Sun rise, beginning and end become clear,
All sins from past births are destroyed just by speaking or listening to this story.

इति श्रीसूर्यपुराण महाकलियुगवर्णनोनामनवमोऽध्यायः ॥
Iti Shri Sūrya Purāṇ Mahā-Kaliyug-varṇanonāma Navamo'dhyāyaḥ.

Thus ends the ninth chapter of the Sūrya Purāṇ,
Titled *"The Great Description of the Age of Kaliyug."*

Chapter 10
The Twelve Forms of the Sun

(Sūrya Dvādaśarūpa Varṇana Nāma Daśamo'dhyāyaḥ)
– Monthly forms of Surya and their corresponding zodiac signs.

Chapter 10 is a detailed exposition on the sacred observances tied to each month of the Hindu calendar in honour of Lord Surya. It reveals how Surya's presence and influence shift through the twelve zodiac signs (*Rāśis*), and how each month holds a specific divine name and virtue associated with the Sun.

The chapter provides prescribed offerings, practices, and benefits for each month:

- Māgha (Aquarius) promotes spiritual purity,
- Phālguna emphasizes milk-based offerings,
- Caitra, Vaiśākha, and others highlight minimal, sattvic diets,
- Special offerings such as kusa grass, clarified butter, sacred ash, and fruits are mentioned.

These month-wise fasts and rituals are meant to align one's body, mind, and soul with Surya's cosmic rhythm. The chapter emphasizes that regular observance ensures health, longevity, and spiritual merit, even helping to eliminate afflictions like leprosy or barrenness described in previous chapters.

It is a spiritual calendar that not only venerates the Sun but also cultivates discipline and gratitude throughout the year. This chapter is especially valuable for devotees who wish to engage in systematic and meaningful worship of Surya over time.

The Power of Monthly Devotion to Surya

बोलीं तबहिं उमा हरषाई ।
दया करहु कछु कहौं गोसाँई ॥
Bolīṁ tabahiṁ Umā haraṣāī,
Dayā karahu kachhu kahoṁ Gosāī.

Then Uma (Parvati) spoke joyfully,
"O Lord, have mercy and tell me more."

जेहि सेवा कर नर सुख पावै ।
ताहि भजे शुभ गति नर पावै ॥
Jehi sevā kar nar sukh pāvai,
Tāhi bhaje śubh gati nar pāvai.

He who serves and worships the Sun attains true happiness,
And by devotion to Him, one reaches the highest spiritual state.

रवि महिमा अति अगम अपारा ।
कहिये नाथ कथा बिस्तारा ॥
Ravi mahimā ati agam apārā,
Kahiye Nāth kathā bistārā.

O Lord, the glory of Ravi (the Sun) is unfathomable and vast,
Please narrate His story in full detail.

जाकी भक्ति मिले सब धानी ।
सो प्रसंग सब कहहु बखानी ॥
Jākī bhakti mile sab dhānī,
So prasang sab kahahu bakhānī.

The one whose devotion grants all wealth and blessings—
Please narrate all the stories related to Him.

अति उत्तम जश रवि अवगाहा ।
सो प्रभु बरनौं सहित उछाहा ॥
Ati uttam jash Ravi avagāhā,
So Prabhu barnaūṁ sahit uchchhāhā.

The supreme glory of Ravi is worth immersing in,
With enthusiasm, I wish to describe that divine Lord.

कंस स्वरूप किमि रूपहिं करहीं ।
किमि शीतल किमि तेजहिं धरहीं ॥
Kaṁs swarūp kimi rūpahiṁ karahīṁ,
Kimi śītal kimi tejahiṁ dharahīṁ?

How does He (Surya), who can take the form of a fierce destroyer like Kansa,
Also appear gentle and cool, and yet bear immense fire and brilliance?

यह प्रति मास कह उदय गोसाँई ।
किमि व्रत कर नर मोक्षहि पाई ॥
Yah prati mās kah uday Gosāī,
Kimi vrat kar nar mokṣahiṁ pāī?

O Lord, tell me how the Sun rises each month,
And how humans may observe fasts to attain liberation (moksha)?

सुनहु सत्य सब कहौं बिचारी ।
जेहि सुनि होय ज्ञान अधिकारी ॥
Sunahu satya sab kahoṁ bichārī,
Jehi suni hoy jñān adhikārī.

Please tell me the absolute truth with reflection and reason,
So that whoever hears it may become a true knower, worthy of wisdom.

असु कहि शिवपद बन्दन कीन्हा ।
हर्षि शम्भु हरि सुमिरन कीन्हा ॥
As kahi Shivpad bandan kīnhā,
Harṣi Śambhu Hari sumiran kīnhā.

Having spoken thus, she bowed at Lord Shiva's feet,
With joy, Shambhu (Shiva) then meditated upon Lord Hari (Vishnu).

दो०- धन्य-धन्य गिरिजा सुनहु, पूजत जग हित लाग ।
रवि चरित्र पावन परम, सुनहु सहित अनुराग ॥
Doha (Couplet):
Dhanya-dhanya Girijā sunahu, pūjat jag hit lāg.
Ravi charitra pāvan param, sunahu sahit anurāg.

O most blessed Girija, listen—
Worship of the Sun is done for the welfare of the world.
His story is supremely pure—
Hear it with devotion and love.

रवि-मंडल कर सुनु बिस्तारा ।
जेहि विधि तन स्थूल अपारा ॥
Ravi-maṇḍal kar sunu bistārā,
Jehi vidhi tan sthūl apārā.

Now hear the full description of the Sun's divine orb (Ravi-maṇḍala),
And the way its vast physical form is structured.

द्वादस सहस्र योजन चहुँ फेरा ।
रवि-मंडल जानहु शुभ डेरा ॥
Dvādas sahasra yojan chahuṁ pherā,
Ravi-maṇḍal jānahu śubh ḍerā.

Its circumference is twelve thousand yojanas,
Know this radiant Sun-orb as a most auspicious realm.

अति उत्तम अति तेज अपारा ।
गये समीप न होय उबारा ॥
Ati uttam ati tej apārā,
Gaye samīp na hoy ubārā.

It is supremely brilliant and
boundless in radiance—
No one can survive upon going
too nearby.

दस सहस्र रवि नयन गिनाये ।
अति विशाल कहि देवन गाये ॥
Das sahasra Ravi nayan ināye,
Ati viśāl kahi devan gāye.

Ten thousand Suns are counted
as its eyes,
It is immensely vast—so say the
Gods in their hymns.

उदय होत त्रिभुवन तम भागे ।
तासन हम नित-नित वर माँगे ॥
Uday hot tribhuvan tam bhāge,
Tāsan ham nit-nit var māṅge.

At sunrise, the darkness of all
three worlds disappears,
And we daily seek blessings from
that source of divine light.

पारब्रह्म साक्षी तेहि जाने ।
सुमिरत हिये ध्यान उर आने ॥
Pārabrahma sākṣhī tehi jāne,
Sumirat hiye dhyān ur āne.

Know that the Sun is the witness-
form of the Supreme Brahman,
Remembering Him draws deep
meditation into one's heart.

उदय होत विधि रूपहिं जानो ।
मध्य विष्णु का रूप बखानो ॥
Uday hot Vidhi rūpahiṁ jāno,
Madhya Viṣṇu kā rūp bakhāno.

At sunrise, recognize Him as the
form of Brahma (Vidhi),
At midday, He takes the glorious
form of Vishnu.

सन्ध्या रूप रुद्र गति केरी ।
तीन काल शुभ मूरति टेरी ॥
Sandhyā rūp Rudra gati kerī,
Tīn kāl śubh mūrti ṭerī.

At dusk, He assumes the form of Rudra (Shiva) and withdraws the day, thus, in all three times (dawn, noon, dusk), He manifests as an auspicious divine form.

यह अनुमान सदा पद बन्दिय ।
निश्चय कर विश्वास अनन्दिय ॥
Yah anumān sadā pad bandiy,
Niśchay kar viśwās ānandiy.

This understanding is a cause for constant reverence,
Believe it with certainty and feel inner joy and bliss.

पावहिं गति ते नर बड़भागी ।
जाके चरन-कमल लव लागी ॥
Pāvahiṁ gati te nar baṛabhāgī,
Jāke charan-kamal lav lāgī.

Those blessed souls who are even slightly devoted to His lotus feet,
Surely attain liberation and a noble spiritual path.

दो०- यहि विधि जानहु हे उमा, रविपूजा जेहि हेतु ।
सिद्ध तासु मनकामना, चारि पदारथ देतु ॥
Doha (Couplet):
Yahi vidhi jānahu he Umā, Ravi-pūjā jehi hetu.
Siddh tāsu mankāmanā, chāri padārath detu.

Know this, O Uma, as the true purpose of Surya worship—
One's desires are fulfilled, and all four aims of life (dharma, artha, kāma, moksha) are granted.

और सुनहु प्रभु की प्रभुताई ।
सूर्य-कथा सब देवन गाई ॥
Aur sunahu Prabhu kī prabhutāī,
Sūrya-kathā sab devan gāī.

Now listen further to the Lord's divine power—
The glories of Surya is sung by all the Gods.

द्वादश तन धरि वेद बखाने ।
द्वादश कथा उद्योग विधाने ॥
Dvādaś tan dhari Ved bakhāne,
Dvādaś kathā udyog vidhāne.

The Sun manifests in twelve forms, as revealed by the Vedas,
And there are twelve sacred stories corresponding to each, detailing His divine acts.

द्वादश मास के द्वादश नामा ।
उदय करे रवि जग सुखधामा ॥
Dvādaś mās ke dvādaś nāmā,
Uday kare Ravi jag sukhadhāmā.

To each of the twelve months corresponds one of these divine names, and Lord Ravi (Surya) rises in each form, bringing joy and prosperity to the world.

माघ मास मासन महँ नीका ।
कह श्रुति सब मासन के टीका ||
Māgh mās māsan maṁh nīkā,
Kah Śruti sab māsan ke ṭīkā.

Among all months, Magha is considered the best,
So say the scriptures in their commentary on each month.

मकर उदय कहि वरुण सुनामा ।
भक्ति ज्ञान ध्यान कर जामा ॥
Makar uday kahi Varuṇ sunāmā,
Bhakti, jñān, dhyān kar jāmā.

When the Sun rises in Capricorn (Makara), He is called Varuṇa,
This is the time to wear the garments of devotion, knowledge, and meditation.

चैत मीन रवि उदय कराहीं ।
नाम देव जग जाने ताहीं ॥
Chait Mīn Ravi uday karāhīṁ,
Nām Dev jag jāne tāhīṁ.

When the Sun rises in Pisces (Meena) during the month of Chaitra,
He is known as Dev, a name recognized throughout the world.

मेष बैसाख भानु जब होई ।
उच्च नाम रवि कहिहैं सोई ।
Meṣ Baisākh Bhānu jab hoī,
Uccha nām Ravi kahihaṁ soī.

When the Sun is in Aries (Mesha) during Baisakh,
He is said to be in exaltation (Uchcha) and is called Ravi.

दो०- इन्द्र नाम व्रत ज्येष्ठ तप, सब प्रकार सुख देहिं ।
रवि आषाढ़ तप कर मिथुन, जासु नाम जप लेहिं ॥
Doha (Couplet):
Indra nām vrat Jyeṣṭh tap, sab prakār sukh dehiṁ,
Ravi Āṣāḍh tap kar Mithun, jāsu nām jap lehiṁ.

In Jyeshtha, the Sun is called Indra; fasting and penance during this month bring all forms of happiness.
In Ashadha, the Sun rises in Gemini (Mithuna) and is known as Tap, whose name is recited with devotion.

सावन कर्क नाम रवि केरा ।
भादौ सिंह भवन का फेरा ॥
Sāvan Karka nām Ravi kerā,
Bhādau Siṁh bhavan kā pherā.

In Shravan, when the Sun is in Cancer (Karka), that is His name;
In Bhadrapada, He resides in Leo (Simha), returning to His own celestial home.

आश्विन कन्या राशि बिराजै ।
सुन नर नित्य नाम शुभ छाजै ॥
Āświn Kanyā rāśi birājai,
Sun nar nitya nām śubh chhājai.

In Ashwin, the Sun resides in Virgo (Kanya Rashi),
Let people listen and recite His name daily, for it brings auspiciousness.

कार्तिक तुला दिवाकर नामा ।
उदय करहि रवि जग सुखधामा ॥
Kārtik Tulā Divākar nāmā,
Uday karahiṁ Ravi jag sukhadhāmā.

In Kartik, when the Sun enters Libra (Tula), He is known as Divakar,
And rises to bring joy and prosperity to the entire world.

मार्गशीर्ष वृश्चिकहिं सोहाई ।
मित्र नाम सब जग सुखदाई ॥
Mārgaśīrṣa Vṛścikahiṁ sohāī,
Mitra nām sab jag sukhadāī.

In Margashirsha, when the Sun is in Scorpio (Vrishchika),
He is called Mitra, the universal friend who brings joy to all.

पौष मास धनु राशि गिनाये ।
विष्णु सनातन नाम कहाये ॥
Pauṣ mās Dhanu rāśi gināye,
Viṣṇu Sanātan nām kahāye.

In the month of Pausha, as the Sun enters Sagittarius (Dhanu Rashi),
He is known as Vishnu, the eternal and ever-present deity.

यहि विधि द्वादश मास के माहीं ।
मास मास प्रति उदय कराहीं ॥
Yahi vidhi dvādaś mās ke māhīṁ,
Mās-mās prati uday karāhīṁ.

Thus, in each of the twelve months,
The Sun rises with a new divine form.

चारों वेद कहै अस बानी ।
मास मास प्रति उदय भवानी ॥
Chāroṁ Ved kahai as bānī,
Mās-mās prati uday Bhavānī.

All four Vedas proclaim this truth—
That each month the Sun rises with divine significance, O Bhavani.

दो०- सुनो उमा यह सकल व्रत, दिनकर याहि बिधान ।
जाहि करे शुभ गति मिले, गावैं वेद पुरान ॥
Doha (Couplet):
Suno Umā yah sakal vrat, Dinkar yāhi bidhān.
Jāhi kare śubh gati mile, gāvaiṁ Ved Purān.

Listen, O Uma, to all these sacred vows (vrats) of Surya, the Sun God.
Whoever performs them attains liberation—so say the Vedas and Puranas.

इतिश्रीसूर्यपुराणे सूर्यवर्णनोनाम दशमोऽध्यायः ॥
Iti Shri Sūrya Purāṇe Sūrya Varṇanonāma Daśamo'dhyāyaḥ.

Thus ends the tenth chapter of the Surya Purana,
Titled *"The Description of the Twelve Forms of Surya."*

CHAPTER 11
RITUALS OF LIGHT

(Vratavidhi Varṇana Nāma Ekādaśo'dhyāyaḥ)
– How to observe Sunday fasts and offer proper worship.

Chapter 11 celebrates the boundless grace, power, and blessings of Lord Surya for those who worship Him with faith and devotion. This chapter affirms that even those facing immense suffering or spiritual ignorance can attain relief, progress, and divine favour through regular and sincere worship of the Sun God.

It continues the dialogue between Lord Shiva and Goddess Parvati (Uma), where Parvati joyfully requests Shiva to elaborate further on the benefits of Surya's worship. Shiva explains how devotees—especially those who fast on Sundays, feed Brahmins, chant the Surya Purana, and maintain purity in thoughts, words, and actions—are guaranteed peace, health, prosperity, and spiritual upliftment.

The chapter also touches on the healing of diseases, removal of sins, and the prosperity gained by offering flower garlands, performing homas (fire offerings), and chanting Surya's names. Most importantly, it reinforces the idea that Surya devotion transcends ritual and leads to inner transformation, liberation (moksha), and divine grace.

This chapter serves as both a spiritual motivation and a practical guide for those seeking fame, well-being, progeny, and salvation, emphasizing that Surya is not merely a celestial force—but a benevolent, responsive deity who empowers human lives.

The Supreme Rewards of Surya Worship

मन स्थिर कर सुनु शैलकुमारी ।
व्रत विधान कहौं बिस्तारी ॥
Man sthir kar sunu Śailkumārī,
Vrat-vidhān kahauṁ bistārī.

Now still your mind and listen, O daughter of the mountains,
I shall explain in detail the rituals and rules of Surya worship (vrat-vidhi).

शनिवार लघु भोजन कीजै ।
आदितवार धरम बहु कीजै ॥
Śanivār laghu bhojan kījai,
Āditvār dharam bahu kījai.

On Saturdays, take light food (as preparation),
And on Sundays, perform various acts of dharma (righteousness).

दन्तकाष्ठ पहिले कर कीजै ।
तब स्नानहिं चित्तहिं दीजै ॥
Dantakāṣṭha pahile kar kījai,
Tab snānahim chittahim dījai.

First, clean the teeth with a twig (dantakaṣṭha),
Then with full focus, proceed to bathe.

उदय होत रवि अंजलि देई ।
सात प्रदक्षिण करिये सोई ॥
Uday hot Ravi añjali deī,
Sāt pradakṣiṇa kariye soī.

At sunrise, offer water (anjali) to Lord Surya,
And then perform seven circumambulations (pradakshina) around Him.

तब धोती अरु लाल उपरना ।
होम करे पढ़ि मन्त्र सपरना ॥
Tab dhotī aru lāl uparnā,
Hom kare paṛhi mantra saparnā.

Wearing a clean dhoti with a red cloth (upper garment),
One should perform a homa (fire offering) while chanting mantras with devotion and clarity.

बन्दि दंडवत रवि कहँ करई ।
दृढ़ विश्वास चित्त महँ धरई ॥
Bandi daṇḍavat Ravi kahṁ karai,
Dṛiḍh viśwās chitt maṁh dharai.

Bow down in full prostration (dandavat) before Lord Surya,
And hold firm faith and concentration in the heart.

अगहन ते यहि व्रतहिं बखानी ।
ताकर विधि अवश्य करि जानी ॥
Aghan te yahi vratahiṁ bakhānī,
Tākar vidhi avaśya kari jānī.

From the month of Aghan (Margashirsha), this vow begins,
Its method must be known and practiced sincerely.

अगहन महँ तुलसीदल खंडित ।
व्रतहिं करे सूक्ष्म ते पण्डित ॥
Aghan maṁh Tulasīdal khaṇḍit,
Vratahiṁ kare sūkṣma te paṇḍit.

In the month of Aghan, the use of broken Tulsi leaves is avoided,
Wise devotees observe the vow with utmost subtlety and purity.

पूष मास गौ घृत फल तीना ।
अति पुनीत काया करि दीन्हा ॥
Pūṣ mās gau-ghṛit phal tīnān,
Ati puneet kāyā kari dīnhā.

In the month of Paush, offer cow ghee and three kinds of fruits,
Thus making the body pure and worthy of the vow.

दो०- माघ मास व्रत जो करे, मुष्टि तीन तिल खाय ।
व्रत विधान जो करहिं नर, रवि लोकन को जाय ॥
Doha (Couplet):
Māgh mās vrat jo kare, muṣṭi tīn til khāy,
Vrat vidhān jo karahiṁ nar, Ravi lokan ko jāy.

Whoever performs the vow in Magha and eats just three pinches of sesame seeds,
And follows the true rituals, that person shall attain the abode of Surya (Sun-loka).

फागुन मास का व्रत सुखदाई ।
क्षीर तीन पल भोजन खाई ।।
Phāgun mās kā vrat sukhadāī,
Kṣhīr tīn pal bhojan khāī.

The vow of Phalgun brings great joy and comfort,
One should eat only three palas (small weights) of milk or milk-based food.

चैत मास कर सुनहु विधाना ।
दही तीन पल अधिक न पाना ॥
Chait mās kar sunahu vidhānā,
Dahī tīn pal adhik na pānā.

Listen to the observance for the month of Chaitra:
Eat only three palas (small measures) of curd—no more than that.

बैसाख गोघृत गोबर आना ।
तीनहिं पल ते अधिक न माना ॥
Baisākh go-ghṛit gobar ānā,
Tīnahīṁ pal te adhik na mānā.

In Baisakh, consume three palas of cow ghee and dried cow dung ash (used for purification);
Do not take more than that.

ज्येष्ठ मास करि यही विधाना । त्रयं अन्जुल करै जल पाना ॥ Jyeṣṭh mās kari yahi vidhānā, Trayaṁ añjul karai jal pānā.	In the month of Jyeshtha, observe the vow by Drinking three handfuls (anjali) of water—nothing else.
मास आषाढ़ व्रत कष्ट धरई । तीन मरिच अवलम्बन करई ॥ Mās Āṣāḍh vrat kaṣṭ dharai, Tīn marich avalamban karai.	The Āṣāḍh month's vow is challenging: One must sustain on three black pepper seeds.
श्रावन मास व्रत रवि नीका । खाँड तीन पल है सबहीं का ॥ Śrāvaṇ mās vrat Ravi nīkā, Khāṇḍ tīn pal hai sabhīṁ kā.	The Shravan month's vow is very dear to Surya: Eat only three palas of sugar (khāṇḍ).
भादो मास अमित सुखदाई । त्रय अंजलि गोमूत्रहिं खाईं ॥ Bhādo mās amit sukhadāī, Traya añjali gomūtrahiṁ khāī.	The vow in Bhadrapada gives immense blessings: Take three handfuls of cow urine as sacred consumption.
आश्विन मास व्रत शुभ जाने । फल केदली के तीन बखाने ॥ Āświn mās vrat śubh jāne, Phal kedalī ke tīn bakhāne.	The Ashwin month's vow is considered very auspicious: One should eat three fruits of the banana plant (including stem or blossom as per custom).

कार्तिक मास व्रत जो करई।
त्रय फल हव्य आन के धरई॥
Kārtik mās vrat jo karaī,
Traya phal havya ān ke dharaī.

Whoever observes the Kartik month fast,
Should offer three types of fruits as sacred oblation (havya).

दो०- यहि विधि बारह मास लगि , व्रत विधान के लीन।
रवि-पूजा विधिवत करहिं, मुनि दुर्लभ सों दीन॥
Doha (Couplet):
Yahi vidhi bārah mās lagi, vrat vidhān ke līn,
Ravi-pūjā vidhivat karahiṁ, muni durlabh soṁ dīn.

Thus, throughout all twelve months, those who follow these vows,
And worship Surya with proper rituals, attain what even sages rarely achieve.

तुम सन सुत विचार नित, कह्यो सो प्रगटे आइ।
अब जो कछु कहिये उमा, सो बरनी हरषाइ॥
Tum san sut vichār nit, kahyo so pragaṭe āi,
Ab jo kachhu kahiye Umā, so barnī harṣāi.

You always reflect on the highest truth, and whatever you say becomes manifest,
Now whatever remains to be said, I shall joyfully express, O Uma.

इति श्रीसूर्यमहापुराणे सूर्यकथावर्णनोनाम एकादशोऽध्यायः ॥

Iti Shri Sūrya Mahāpurāṇe Sūrya Kathā Varṇanonāma Ekādaśo'dhyāyaḥ.

Thus ends the 11th chapter of the Surya Mahapurana,
Titled *"The Description of Surya's Glorious Stories."*

CHAPTER 12
THE GRACE OF SURYA

(Umā-Maheśvara Samvāda Nāma Dvādaśo'dhyāyaḥ)
– Final reflections and praises, ending the sacred tale.

Chapter 12 concludes the *Surya Puran* with a sacred and uplifting dialogue between Lord Shiva and Goddess Uma. Having heard the profound tales of Surya's power, Uma praises the Lord and expresses her joy and gratitude for being guided toward divine knowledge. She acknowledges that the illusions of Maya and worldly suffering have been lifted through the grace of this narration.

Lord Shiva emphasizes that those who regularly read, recite, or even listen to the stories of Surya with attention and devotion will be blessed with all their desires fulfilled. Worship of Surya is said to eliminate suffering, bestow health and prosperity, ensure progeny for the childless, success for the job-seeker, and peace for the disturbed.

This chapter reiterates the immense spiritual merit gained by observing Surya fasts, maintaining discipline, and practicing charity—especially on Sundays. It affirms that even sages and Gods revere Surya, and thus, humans who follow His path with sincerity are assured divine blessings.

The sacred dialogue ends with a benediction: those who read this Purana with devotion will never be bound by worldly pain, and Lord Surya will reside in their hearts forever.

The Sacred Dialogue and the Fruits of Devotion

सो सुन उमा हर्ष अति भई ।
माया मोह व्यथा सब गई ॥
So sun Umā harṣ ati bhaī,
Māyā moha vyathā sab gaī.

Upon hearing this, Uma was filled with immense joy,
All delusion, illusion, and sorrow were completely gone.

धन्य धन्य सुनु शंकर स्वामी ।
कथा कहौं नित हर्षित बानी ॥
Dhanya dhanya sunu Śaṅkar Swāmī,
Kathā kahoṁ nit harṣit bānī.

Blessed, blessed are you, O Lord Shankar—
Let me speak this sacred story daily with joy in my voice.

जे करता रवि पूजन लोगा ।
करहिं आनन्द मिटहिं सब रोगा ।
Je kartā Ravi pūjan logā,
Karahiṁ ānand miṭahiṁ sab rogā.

Those who perform Sun worship with devotion,
Live in joy and have all their diseases removed.

कथा और पुनि कहौं गुसाँई ।
सो तुम और कछु करौ सहाई ॥
Kathā aur puni kahoṁ Gusāī,
So tum aur kachhu karahu sahāī.

O Lord, please tell more of this sacred story,
And bless me further with Your support and guidance.

दो०- शिवा शम्भु संवाद यह, पढ़े धरे चित ध्यान ।
ताकी सब मनकामना, पुरवहिं श्री भगवान ॥
Doha (Couplet):
Śivā Śambhu samvāda yah, paṛhe dhare chit dhyān,
Tākī sab manakāmanā, puravahiṁ Shri Bhagwān.

Whoever reads and reflects on this dialogue between Shiva and Uma,
Shall have all their heartfelt wishes fulfilled by Lord Surya Himself.

इतिश्री सूर्यमहापुराणे सूर्यमाहात्म्ये उमामहेश्वरसम्वादे
सूर्यकथा वर्णनोनाम द्वादशोऽध्यायः ॥ समाप्त ॥
Iti Shri Sūrya Mahāpurāṇe Sūrya Māhātmye Umā-Maheśvara Samvāde
Sūrya Kathā Varṇanonāma Dvādaśo'dhyāyaḥ ll Samāpt ll

Thus ends the 12th chapter of the Surya Mahapurana,
In the section of Surya Mahatmya, within the sacred dialogue of Uma and Maheshwara (Shiva),
Titled *"The Description of the Sun's Divine Stories."* —End—

Astrological Benefits of Reciting the Surya Puran

1. Fame and Respect:
Surya Dev is the giver of brilliance and glory. Worshiping him through the Surya Puran is said to grant public recognition, honour, and admiration—especially to those in leadership, arts, or public life.

2. Strength and Confidence:
The Sun represents willpower, courage, and inner strength. Regular recitation strengthens mental resolve, leadership qualities, and the ability to face adversity boldly.

3. Career and Job Stability:
Surya governs the soul and karma. His grace is believed to remove obstacles, enhance focus and discipline, and attract favourable opportunities, helping one thrive in career or business.

4. Fulfils Desires and Grants Success:
The Puran states that sincere readers, especially those who observe Sunday fasts and rituals, have their desires fulfilled—including material gains and professional growth.

5. Healing of Diseases and Ailments:
The text emphasizes that worship of Surya Dev—especially as prescribed in the Puran—can cure conditions like leprosy, blindness, and infertility, symbolizing both physical and spiritual healing.

Shree Aditya Hridaya Stotram

ततो युद्धपरिश्रान्तं समरे चिन्तया स्थितम् ।
रावणं चाग्रतो दृष्ट्वा युद्धाय समुपस्थितम् ॥१॥

Tato yuddha-pariśrāntaṁ samare cintayā sthitam I
Rāvaṇaṁ cāgrato dṛṣṭvā yuddhāya samupasthitam II1 II

दैवतैश्च समागम्य द्रष्टुमभ्यागतो रणम् ।
उपगम्याब्रवीद्राममगस्त्यो भगवानृषिः ॥२॥

Daivataiśca samāgamya draṣṭumabhyāgato raṇam I
Upagamyābravīdrāmam agastyo bhagavānṛṣiḥ II2 II

राम राम महाबाहो शृणु गुह्यं सनातनम् ।
येन सर्वानरीन् वत्स समरे विजयिष्यसे ॥३॥

Rāma rāma mahābāho śṛṇu guhyaṁ sanātanam I
Yena sarvānarīn vatsa samare vijayiṣyase II3 II

आदित्यहृदयं पुण्यं सर्वशत्रुविनाशनम् ।
जयावहं जपं नित्यमक्षयं परमं शिवम् ॥४॥

Āditya-hṛdayaṁ puṇyaṁ sarva-śatru-vināśanam I
Jayāvahaṁ japaṁ nityam akṣayaṁ paramaṁ śivam II4 II

सर्वमङ्गलमाङ्गल्यं सर्वपापप्रणाशनम् ।
चिन्ताशोकप्रशमनमायुर्वर्धनमुत्तमम् ॥५॥

Sarva-maṅgala-māṅgalyaṁ sarva-pāpa-praṇāśanam I
Cintā-śoka-praśamanam āyurvardhanamuttamam II5 II

रश्मिमन्तं समुद्यन्तं देवासुरनमस्कृतम् ।
पूजयस्व विवस्वन्तं भास्करं भुवनेश्वरम् ॥६॥

Raśmi-mantaṁ samudyantaṁ devāsura-namaskṛtam I
Pūjayasva vivasvantaṁ bhāskaraṁ bhuvaneśvaram II6 II

सर्वदेवात्मको ह्येष तेजस्वी रश्मिभावनः ।
एष देवासुरगणाँल्लोकान् पाति गभस्तिभिः ॥७॥

Sarva-devātmako hy eṣa tejasvī raśmi-bhāvanaḥ I
Eṣa devāsura-gaṇān lokān pāti gabhastibhiḥ II7 II

एष ब्रह्मा च विष्णुश्च शिवः स्कन्दः प्रजापतिः ।
महेन्द्रो धनदः कालो यमः सोमो ह्यपाम्पतिः ॥८॥

Eṣa brahmā ca viṣṇuśca śivaḥ skandaḥ prajāpatiḥ I
Mahendro dhanadaḥ kālo yamaḥ somo hy apāmpatiḥ II8 II

पितरो वसवः साध्या अश्विनौ मरुतो मनुः ।
वायुर्वह्निः प्रजाः प्राण ऋतुकर्ता प्रभाकरः ॥९॥

Pitaro vasavaḥ sādhya aśvinau maruto manuḥ I
Vāyurvahniḥ prajāḥ prāṇa ṛtukartā prabhākaraḥ II9 II

आदित्यः सविता सूर्यः खगः पूषा गभस्तिमान् ।
सुवर्णसदृशो भानुर्हिरण्यरेता दिवाकरः ॥१०॥

Ādityaḥ savitā sūryaḥ khagaḥ pūṣā gabhastimān I
Suvarṇa-sadṛśo bhānuḥ hiraṇyaretā divākaraḥ II10 II

हरिदश्वः सहस्रार्चिः सप्तसप्तिर्मरीचिमान् ।
तिमिरोन्मथनः शम्भुस्त्वष्टा मार्तण्डकोंऽशुमान् ॥११॥

Haridaśvaḥ sahasrārciḥ sapta-saptir marīcimān I
Timiro-nmathanaḥ śambhus tvaṣṭā mārtaṇḍako'ṁśumān II11 II

हिरण्यगर्भः शिशिरस्तपनो ऽहस्करो रविः ।
अग्निगर्भोऽदितेः पुत्रः शङ्खः शिशिरनाशनः ॥१२॥

Hiraṇya-garbhaḥ śiśiras tapano'has-karo raviḥ I
Agni-garbho'diteḥ putraḥ śaṅkhaḥ śiśira-nāśanaḥ II12 II

व्योमनाथस्तमोभेदी ऋग्यजुः सामपारगः ।
घनवृष्टिरपां मित्रो विन्ध्यवीथीप्लवङ्गमः ॥१३॥

Vyomanāthas tamo-bhedī ṛg-yajuḥ-sāma-pāragaḥ I
Ghana-vṛṣṭir apāṁ mitro vindhya-vīthī-plavaṅgamaḥ II13 II

आतपी मण्डली मृत्युः पिङ्गलः सर्वतापनः ।
कविर्विश्वो महातेजा रक्तः सर्वभवोद्भवः ॥१४॥

Ātapī maṇḍalī mṛtyuḥ piṅgalaḥ sarva-tāpanaḥ I
Kavirviśvo mahā-tejā raktaḥ sarva-bhavodbhavaḥ II14 II

नक्षत्रग्रहताराणामधिपो विश्वभावनः ।
तेजसामपि तेजस्वी द्वादशात्मन् नमोऽस्तुते ॥१५॥

Nakṣatra-graha-tārāṇām adhipo viśva-bhāvanaḥ I
Tejasāmapi tejasvī dvādaśātman namo'stute II15 II

नमः पूर्वाय गिरये पश्चिमायाद्रये नमः ।
ज्योतिर्गणानां पतये दिनाधिपतये नमः ॥१६॥

Namaḥ pūrvāya giraye paścimāyādraye namaḥ I
Jyotir-gaṇānāṁ pataye dinādhipataye namaḥ II16 II

जयाय जयभद्राय हर्यश्वाय नमो नमः ।
नमो नमः सहस्रांशो आदित्याय नमो नमः ॥१७॥

Jayāya jaya-bhadrāya haryaśvāya namo namaḥ I
Namo namaḥ sahasrāṁśo ādityāya namo namaḥ II 17 II

नम उग्राय वीराय सारङ्गाय नमो नमः ।
नमः पद्मप्रबोधाय प्रचण्डाय नमोऽस्तुते ॥१८॥

Nama ugrāya vīrāya sāraṅgāya namo namaḥ I
Namaḥ padma-prabodhāya pracaṇḍāya namo'stute II 18 II

ब्रह्मेशानाच्युतेशाय सूरायादित्यवर्चसे ।
भास्वते सर्वभक्षाय रौद्राय वपुषे नमः ॥१९॥

Brahmeśānācyuteśāya sūrāyāditya-varcase I
Bhāsvate sarva-bhakṣāya raudrāya vapuṣe namaḥ II 19 II

तमोघ्नाय हिमघ्नाय शत्रुघ्नायामितात्मने ।
कृतघ्नघ्नाय देवाय ज्योतिषां पतये नमः ॥२०॥

Tamo-ghnāya hima-ghnāya śatru-ghnāyāmitātmane I
Kṛtaghna-ghnāya devāya jyotiṣāṁ pataye namaḥ II 20 II

तप्तचामीकराभाय हरये विश्वकर्मणे ।
नमस्तमोऽभिनिघ्नाय रुचये लोकसाक्षिणे ॥२१॥

Tapta-cāmīkara-ābhāya haraye viśvakarmaṇe I
Namas tamo'bhi-nighnāya rucaye loka-sākṣiṇe II21 II

नाशयत्येष वै भूतं तमेष सृजति प्रभुः ।
पायत्येष तपत्येष वर्षत्येष गभस्तिभिः ॥२२॥

Nāśayaty eṣa vai bhūtaṁ tameṣa sṛjati prabhuḥ I
Pāyaty eṣa tapatyeṣa varṣaty eṣa gabhastibhiḥ II22 II

एष सुप्तेषु जागर्ति भूतेषु परिनिष्ठितः ।
एष एवाग्निहोत्रं च फलं चैवाग्निहोत्रिणाम् ॥ २३॥

Eṣa suptēṣu jāgarti bhūtēṣu pariniṣṭhitaḥ I
Eṣa evāgnihotraṁ ca phalaṁ caivāgnihōtriṇām II23 II

वेदाश्च क्रतवश्चैव क्रतूनां फलमेव च ।
यानि कृत्यानि लोकेषु सर्व एष रविः प्रभुः ॥ २४॥

Vēdāśca kratavaścaiva kratūnāṁ phalamēva ca I
Yāni kṛtyāni lōkēṣu sarva ēṣa raviḥ prabhuḥ II24 II

एनमापत्सु कृच्छ्रेषु कान्तारेषु भयेषु च ।
कीर्तयन् पुरुषः कश्चिन्नावसीदति राघव ॥२५॥

Enam āpatsu kṛcchreṣu kāntāreṣu bhayeṣu ca I

Kīrtayan puruṣaḥ kaścin nāvasīdati rāghava II25 II

पूजयस्वैनमेकाग्रो देवदेवं जगत्पतिम् ।
एतत्त्रिगुणितं जप्त्वा युद्धेषु विजयिष्यसि ॥२६॥

Pūjayasvainam ekāgro deva-devaṁ jagat-patim I

Etat-triguṇitaṁ japtvā yuddheṣu vijayiṣyasi II26 II

अस्मिन्क्षणे महाबाहो रावणं त्वं वधिष्यसि ।
एवमुक्त्वा तदाऽगस्त्यो जगाम च यथागतम् ॥ २७॥

Asmin kṣaṇe mahābāho rāvaṇaṁ tvaṁ vadhiṣyasi I

Evam uktvā tadā'gastyo jagāma ca yathāgatam II27 II

एतच्छ्रुत्वा महातेजा नष्टशोकोऽभवत् तदा ।
धारयामास सुप्रीतो राघवः प्रयतात्मवान् ॥२८॥

Etac chrutvā mahā-tejā naṣṭa-śoko'bhavat tadā I

Dhārayāmāsa suprīto rāghavaḥ prayatātmavān II28 II

आदित्यं प्रेक्ष्य जप्त्वेदं परं हर्षमवाप्तवान् ।
त्रिराचम्य शुचिर्भूत्वा धनुरादाय वीर्यवान् ॥२९॥

Ādityaṁ prekṣya japtvedaṁ paraṁ harṣam avāptavān |

Trir ācamya śucir bhūtvā dhanur ādāya vīryavān ||29||

रावणं प्रेक्ष्य हृष्टात्मा युद्धाय समुपागमत् ।
सर्व यत्नेन महता वधे तस्य धृतोऽभवत् ॥ ३०॥

Rāvaṇaṁ prekṣya hṛṣṭātmā yuddhāya samupāgamat |

Sarva yatnena mahatā vadhe tasya dhṛto'bhavat ||30||

अथ रविरवदन्निरीक्ष्य रामं मुदितमनाः परमं प्रहृष्यमाणः ।
निशिचरपतिसंक्षयं विदित्वा सुरगणमध्यगतो वचस्त्वरेति ॥३१॥

Atha ravir avadan nirikṣya rāmaṁ mudita-manāḥ paramaṁ prahṛṣyamāṇaḥ |
Niśicara-pati-saṁkṣayaṁ viditvā suragaṇa-madhyagato vacas tvareti ||31||

~ ~ ~ ~

May the divine light of Surya guide your path, bless your life, and awaken the radiance within.

Om Suryaya Namah

www.ingramcontent.com/pod-product-compliance
Ingram Content Group UK Ltd.
Pitfield, Milton Keynes, MK11 3LW, UK
UKHW021337190726
13845UKWH00027B/603